To all the Chen Family:
God & and, you'll love.
S. Jo. Palmeri

TALES
FROM
THE BARBER SHOP

© Copyright 2005 Josephine Teresa Palmeri.
All rights reserved. No part of this publication may be reproduced, stored in a retrieval system, or transmitted, in any form or by any means, electronic, mechanical, photocopying, recording, or otherwise, without the written prior permission of the author.

Note for Librarians: A cataloguing record for this book is available from Library and Archives Canada at www.collectionscanada.ca/amicus/index-e.html
ISBN 1-4120-5131-2

Printed in Victoria, BC, Canada. Printed on paper with minimum 30% recycled fibre. Trafford's print shop runs on "green energy" from solar, wind and other environmentally-friendly power sources.

Offices in Canada, USA, Ireland and UK
This book was published *on-demand* in cooperation with Trafford Publishing. On-demand publishing is a unique process and service of making a book available for retail sale to the public taking advantage of on-demand manufacturing and Internet marketing. On-demand publishing includes promotions, retail sales, manufacturing, order fulfilment, accounting and collecting royalties on behalf of the author.

Book sales for North America and international:
Trafford Publishing, 6E–2333 Government St.,
Victoria, BC V8T 4P4 CANADA
phone 250 383 6864 (toll-free 1 888 232 4444)
fax 250 383 6804; email to orders@trafford.com
Book sales in Europe:
Trafford Publishing (UK) Ltd., Enterprise House, Wistaston Road Business Centre,
Wistaston Road, Crewe, Cheshire CW2 7RP UNITED KINGDOM
phone 01270 251 396 (local rate 0845 230 9601)
facsimile 01270 254 983; orders.uk@trafford.com
Order online at:
trafford.com/05-0026

10 9 8 7 6 5 4 3 2 1

TALES FROM THE BARBER SHOP

✂ ✂ ✂

100 Jokes

of

Anthony "Tony Palma" Palmeri,

Barber and Joy-Giver

A Glimpse of His Soul and His Wit

✂ ✂ ✂

By

Sister Jo Palmeri, MPF

*Illustrations by Sister Jo Palmeri, MPF,
and Jack Murphy*

CONTENTS

Preface	9
The Bald Barber: How Tony Got Started	10
Aunt Filomena & Uncle Nicola - The Italian Stories	13
Tony's Irish Stories	16
Tony's Uncle Joe	21
Tony's Famous "Peanuts & Popcorn" Story	27
Tony's Church Jokes	29
Tony's School Jokes	34
Miscellaneous Jokes	39
Make Fun of Yourself, Not Others	45
Tony's "Hair-Raising" Miracle	48
Family Photos	50
How Tony Saved the Drowning Dog	56
Today's Spoiled Kids	58
Tony's Magic	61
Tonsorial Treats	62

The Orphans' Haircuts	64
Wisdom & Brains But No Diploma	65
"Wasting Time" With God	69
Nanna's Subway Miracle	71
Growing In Love	77
Tony & Pittston: A Mutual Love	79
Earthly Father--Image of God?	86
Jokes in the Cemetery	90
Jokes on a Deathbed	93

✂ ✂ ✂ ✂ ✂

MY DEEPEST GRATITUDE TO:

✂ Sr. Ascenza Tizzano, MPF, Provincial Superior of our Religious Teachers Filippini, for her many years of affirmation and for her "go-ahead" for *Tales from the Barber Shop.*

✂ Mrs. Peggy Murphy, of Villa Walsh Academy, Morristown, NJ, for her joy and precious volunteer gift of final layout, and to her husband, Jack, for his artistic talent. Without the work of our benefactors Peggy and Jack, this book might still be a three-ring binder.

✂ Sr. Margherita Marchione, MPF, my religious community's prolific writer, for her repeated encouragement, "Dear, write the joke book."

✂ Santina Palmeri Lonergan, my baby sister and joy of my childhood, who lived these pages with me.

✂ My godchild, Judith Faye Fretz, and friends Rose D'Andrea and Helen Miller.

✂ The good people of Pittston, Pennsylvania, especially my friends from St. Rocco's Parish, whose kindness and spirit I have absorbed over a lifetime; to Joe Ranieli, Jr., Executive Producter and Host of radio's popular *"Bocci Alley,"* of the Baccala Network, for his love for Tony Palma, and to his parents, Joe and Theresa.

✂ Kevin Heitz, Editor of *Ambassador* Magazine, National Italian-American Federation, 1860 Nineteenth Street NS, Washington, DC, 20009, for permission to quote from "Nanna's Subway Miracle," from the Summer 2000 Issue.

✂ Pittston, PA's *Sunday Dispatch*: Tom Bubul's permission to quote from February 12 and April 2, 1978 issues; Billy Watson, Former *Dispatch* Editor, of happy memory who featured Tony Palma stories in *"Local Chatter;"* Ed Philbin for his calls and encouragement.

PREFACE

"Tell us one of your Dad's jokes," people often say to me. "Why don't you write them all down in a book?"

Tony "Palma" Palmeri, beloved barber of Pittston, PA, entertained "off the cuff," a natural gift from God; his jokes were never written down. He kept a shoebox of index cards with cue words. For each banquet, he'd put some cards in his pocket and take a quick peek before approaching the mike. Only Mom, my sister Santina, and I knew what the cue words meant: "Peanuts and Popcorn," "Little Boy Cursing," "Beer and Flashlights."

The shoebox has been lost, but I had heard Dad tell his stories for decades. I have tried to recall 100 from memory, oral tradition passed down from Father to Daughter.

At last, here's the book, for the enjoyment of those who knew and loved Tony, and for those who will meet him through these pages.

This labor of love is dedicated to the memory of our beloved parents, Anthony and Josephine Manganaro Palmeri, who taught their daughters, by word and example, the most important things in life.

THE BALD BARBER:

HOW TONY GOT STARTED

"Hey, Baldy! Get out of the sun! The reflection's blinding me!" shouted my Dad's friend. "Shut up, I had a crew cut once...but the crew bailed out!" came his quick reply, with gales of laughter from bystanders. This was one of my earliest memories of my Dad: young, handsome, dynamic—and bald. His premature hair loss drew more teasing because of his job: Tony Palmeri was a barber! The butt of constant pranks and teasing, Tony, a gifted storyteller, joked right back, building a repertoire about his head.

"I had a crew cut once, but the crew bailed out.

I had hair like snow once; somebody shoveled it off.

My wife gave me a comb for Christmas,
I'll never *part* with it.

I'll let you in on a secret: I'm not really bald;
I just have a *very* high forehead.

Some men have a beautiful head of **hair**.
I have a beautiful head of **skin**.

So what's the big deal? In the morning, you use a comb...
and I use a washcloth."

Tony told these jokes to his customers in the barber shop, to friends at church, to the neighbors. One day a friend said, "Tony, at our Boy Scout banquet next week, we need a humorist. Will you tell jokes about your bald head and make everyone laugh?"

Dad was delighted! Many of his Pittston friends were in the audience, and he brought the house down that night! The Troop Leader handed him a check—his first as a professional comedian!

Word spread. Our *Sunday Dispatch* wrote about the local barber who stole the show. Dad got more and more job offers throughout Greater Pittston Area: Communion breakfasts, Knights of Columbus, parish socials, and his largest job, a banquet for Governor Scranton of Pennsylvania.

He soon became famous as *Tony Palma* in Pennsylvania's Wyoming and Lackawanna Valleys. His name appeared in the papers so often that one January the *Sunday Dispatch* joked in their "Ramblin' Round Our Town" column, that *Dispatch* Editor Billy Watson had made a New Year's Resolution to hold down the use of Tony Palma's name to only five times a year."

As his fame spread, he had business cards made:

TONY PALMA PALMERI
Clean Wholesome Humor
"Laughter is the best medicine."

Dad believed that a truly talented comedian doesn't hurt others. He never joked about fat people, stutterers, or physical handicaps. "If even **one** person in the audience is suffering because of your joke, it's not worth it," he said. "Make fun of **yourself** instead." And he did!

"Ladies and Gentlemen, I'll never forget the first time I found a bald spot on top of my head. I rushed to a New York theatrical agency and said, "Quick, give me a wig!" They said, "No, Mister, the spot's too small. You need what we call in show business, a ***doily***." So I got a doily.

In one year, the bald spot grew around the doily. I rushed back to NY and said, "Quick, I need a bigger doily." "No," they said, 'You need what we call in show business a ***rug***."

So I got a rug. A year later the bald spot grew around the rug. I went to NY and said, "What do I need now?" They said, "Mister, you need **wall-to-wall carpeting**!"

"Yesterday my little daughter Santina was eating her cornflakes and staring at my head:

Santina: "Mommy, how come Daddy has no hair?"

Mommy: (*kindly*) Well, honey, Daddy is very smart. He uses his brains a lot. And when you use your brains, your hair just doesn't grow any more.

Santina: Then, Mommy…how come you have so MUCH hair?

Mommy: Honey, eat your corn flakes and shut up!

Tony was man enough to stand up for what he believed in. The committee chairman of a local men's club once invited him as humorist, but requested that he tell only risqué stories. Tony declined, but promised that he could make the audience laugh without using off-color jokes. The chairman left the barber shop in a huff with, "Go entertain some Sunday School!"

Dad was vindicated a month later at a huge Diocesan banquet, where the audience howled with laughter and gave him a long, loud ovation. The Bishop went to the mike and said, "Tony, you are truly a **gifted** comedian. I've never heard a crowd laugh so long and so loud at **clean** stories. Those with true talent never have to stoop to crude jokes for shock value. God has blessed you with an innate gift for making people laugh."

Of course, the *Dispatch* picked up the story and Dad's fame as a "truly gifted comedian" circulated. Tony fondly remembered that night as his highest tribute.

✂ ✂ ✂ ✂ ✂

AUNT FILOMENA & UNCLE NICOLA – The Italian Stories

At Irish banquets, Tony changed these names to Michael and Kathleen; for Polish audiences, Stanley and Sophie. He could imitate many accents and switch from one to another easily.

My Uncle Nicola & Aunt Filomena were happily married for 50 years, but once in a while they had a fight and said things they didn't mean:

Filomena (crying): You no love-a me no more. Last-a night you **cursed** me in your sleep.

Nicola: Who said I was-a sleepin'?

F: I should-a listened to my mother. She WARNED me not to marry you!

N: Wait a minute! You mean your mother tried to STOP you from-a marrying me?

F: (viciously) YES!

N: (slaps his forehead) Mamma Mia! How I *misjudged* that good woman!

F: Before we got married, you **lied**! You said you was-a rich. You said you was-a *well off*!

N: I *was*-a well-off! But I didn't *know* it!

F: You said, "Filomena, marry me, and I give-a you candlelight & wine." All I ever got from you was BEER and FLASHLIGHTS!"

F: You said, "Filomena, marry me and in **no tim**e you'll be happy!"

So I married you! And at **no time** have I been happy!

F: And you always say nasty things about-a my poor mother.

N: Eh, **when** do I say nasty things about-a your mother?

F: Remember last week when that big clock fell off-a the wall and it smashed in a million pieces? I said, "Ooh, if that clock had fallen ten minutes sooner, it would-a hit my poor mother right on the head!" And you said, " I always knew that darn clock was slow!"

F: And you always insult me! You call me "dumb green horn."

N: Well, you talk so stupid! Remember on the train, on our honeymoon? The train came to a quick stop, and you asked the conductor, "Eh, why you stop-a the train?" And the conductor say, "The train hit a cow." And then you say, "Awww, the poor cow. Was it on the tracks?" And the conductor he say, "No, Lady, we chased up a field after it!"

N: And on the train, they rent pillows. The boy was-a yelling, "Pillows! Pillows!" And you say, "How much-a?" And he say, "50 cents each." And you say, "Oh, give me half a dozen. I no canna buy that cheap in the store!"

N: Filomena, you remember on our honeymoon, I fell in the bathtub, I hit my head, and I was unconscious for 3 days? Well, Filomena, I tell-a you, those was the 3 happiest days of my whole married life!

✂

Once after a fight, Nicola went out to play cards. Later he got hungry and called to see if Filomena was still mad at him.

Nicola: Filomena, what-a you cooking for supper?

Filomena: Poison!

Nicola: Then, just-a make-a one portion. I'm-a not comin' home.

✂

Once Mrs. Merlucci and Filomena had a fight. In church that Sunday, the priest gave an inspiring talk on forgiveness. Filomena decided she would make up with Mrs. Merlucci right after Mass.

Filomena: Hello, Mrs. Merlucci! How nice-a you look! Like a beautiful young girl.

Mrs. M: (nose in air) Well, I'm-a sorry, I no can-a say the same thing about-a YOU!

Filomena: Oh no? Well, you COULD, if you was-a bigga liar like-a ME!

✂ ✂ ✂ ✂ ✂

TONY'S IRISH STORIES

At St. Patrick's Day banquets, Tony changed the Italian Nicola and Filomena stories to Michael and Kathleen, adding jokes he had learned from his many Irish friends:

Kathleen and Michael, after 40 years in America, took a boat trip back to Ireland to visit relatives. Poor Michael got so seasick, that he prepared for death:

Michael: Kathleen, I know I'll die before we get there. And I'm asking you **one favor**. Bury me in Ireland.

Kathleen: Michael, why do you want to be buried in Ireland?

Michael: Because I couldn't stand this trip back again, dead or alive.

✂

Kathleen had deep respect for educated people. One morning she couldn't wake Michael—he lay there like a corpse. Frightened, she called the doctor, who shook his head and said, "Mrs. O'Malley, I'm sorry to tell you your husband is dead." From the bed came a weak voice, "I am **NOT** dead!" Kathleen said, "Be quiet, Michael! The good doctor knows more than you do."

✂

Kathleen O'Malley was so kind, she could never speak ill of anyone. At every wake, she would stand before the coffin and tell all the virtues of the deceased. When the town villain died, everyone was waiting to see what Mrs. O'Malley could possibly say about this bad character. She stood before the coffin, prayed, then said, "Glory be to God, wasn't he a fine whistler?"

Someone said, "Mrs. O'Malley, I bet you could think of something good to say about the **devil**." She smiled, "Well, you've got to admit, he's a hard worker!"

✂

Actually, Mrs. O'Malley did say something negative only once, when her daughter-in-law named the first grandchild.

Kathleen: Michael, what is she naming the baby?
Michael: Now, don't go interfering. She's naming her Hazel.
Kathleen: Aw, glory be to God, all the beautiful Irish saints' names, and she names the baby after a nut!

✂

Michael sometimes drank too much, and Kathleen asked the priest for help. Father thought a good scare might cure Michael. He told Kathleen, "Next time he's drunk, dress up in a devil costume, and say you'll take his soul if he keeps this up." Kathleen did so. As Michael opened his back door in the twilight, he saw the devil sitting at the kitchen table, and jumped in fright.

Michael: (shaking) Who are YOU?
Kathleen: (in a deep voice) I'm the DEVIL!
Michael: Glad to meet you. I married your sister.

✂

Michael was walking unsteadily with one foot on the curb and one foot in the gutter.

Cop: Hey, you've got one foot on the curb, and one in the gutter. You're drunk!
Michael: Oh, thank God! I thought I was crippled.

✂

The Irish cop was trying to save a man ready to jump from a bridge.

Cop: Come down from there. Do it for your dear mother.
Man: Don't have no mother.
Cop: Do it for your wife and kids.
Man: Don't have no wife and kids.
Cop: Then do it for the love of the Pope.
Man: Who's the Pope?
Cop: Who's the Pope! Jump, you Englishman. Jump!

✂

Two intoxicated men went to a wake. Instead of the coffin, they stood before the piano to pray. Pat turned to Mike and said, "Sure and didn't he have a fine set of teeth?"

✂

A man, hit by a truck during a blizzard on a bitterly cold night, kept repeating, "Call me a rabbi. Call me a rabbi." The rabbi came and leaned over the victim:

Rabbi: "What is your name, my good man?"
Man: James Michael Timothy Patrick O'Brien.
Rabbi: Why, it's a Catholic priest you want!
Man: Oh, no, Rabbi. I'd never get the good Father out of bed on a night like this!

✂

Michael's mother-in-law finally left after a 6-month visit! He met a friend:

Friend: "Hey, Mike, how come your hands are so dirty?"
Mike: "I just put my mother-in-law on the train. She's going back home."
Friend: "So why are your hands all black?
Mike: "I patted the engine."

✂

Patrick had a lot of fluid in his lungs. One night his wife called the doctor.

Doctor: "Fluid in the lungs. I'm going to have to tap him."
Bridget: "Oh, no, Doctor, please don't do that!
Doctor: "Why not?"
Bridget: Anything tapped at night in this house never lasts until morning!"

✂

Patrick called his best friend to his bedside. "Dennis," he said, "I'm dying and I know it. Here's $50. On the way to the cemetery, buy all my friends a drink at Duffy's Tavern."

Dennis: What do you mean on the way to the cemetery? We always buy drinks on the way back."

Patrick: Use your brains, you ee-jit! I won't be with ye on the way back!

✂

Bridget was sick one Sunday, so Tim went to Mass without her. On his return, she asked what the sermon was about. Tim, a man of a few words, said, "Sin."

Bridget: "And what did Father say about sin?"
Tim: "He's against it."
The one-sided conversation continued:
Bridget: Was Mrs. McCarthy at Mass, Tim?
Tim: I dunno.
Bridget: Was Mrs. O'Riley there?
Tim: Uh…yeah, I think so.
Bridget: Was she wearing that silly big straw hat of hers?
Tim: I didn't notice.
Bridget: Hmphh! A lot of good it does you to go to Mass!

✂

Tales from the Barbershop

At communion breakfasts, Tony often told this story:

A young man named Jim loved to attend daily Mass, but couldn't. Father of a large family and a hard worker, Jim had to be at his job at 6:30 a.m.

"Since I pass the church on my way to work, I can at least stop in for a second," he decided. And it became a lifelong habit. Each morning, Jim had just enough time to open the church doors, genuflect near the back row, look at the tabernacle, and whisper, "Jesus, this is Jim."

One day Jim was struck by a car, and lay dying in the street. Someone immediately called the ambulance and his parish priest. Jim died just as the ambulance arrived.

Moments before, kneeling by his side, the priest had given him Holy Communion.

As the Sacred Host was placed on his lips, the dying man heard a loving voice whisper, "Jim….this is Jesus."

✂ ✂ ✂ ✂ ✂

 # TONY'S UNCLE JOE

Although we did have an Uncle Joe, these jokes are fiction. People at parties often begged, "Tony, tell about your Uncle Joe!" Later, more names were added, like Luigi and Vincenzo.

Tony: Uncle Joe, how did you like your cruise to Italy?

Joe: Oh, To-nee, beautiful-a boat! Like a palace on the water. But one thing I no like! The automatic washers on the wall.

Tony: Uncle Joe, those weren't washing machines! Those were portholes.

Joe: Porta-hole? No wonder I never got my shirts back.

✂

Tony took Uncle Joe to the New York Automat for lunch and gave him $5 worth of quarters. Joe was fascinated to see the food "come out of those little windows." When Tony returned, Joe had 13 pieces of apple pie on his tray.

Tony: Uncle Joe, *what are you doing with 13 pieces of apple pie?*

Joe: Eh, I no can-a quit while I'm winning!

✂

Uncle Joe: To-nee, you know what-sa matter with the world? The man, he-sa no more the boss. But in my house, I'm-a still the boss. I give you one example: Last-a night I come home. I find no hot water. I yell at my wife, I bang-a my fist, and in 20 minutes, I got plenty of hot water!.....If SHE thinks I'm gonna wash-a the dishes in cold water, she's-a crazy!

Tony: Oh, so you're the boss, but you wash the dishes for your wife?

Joe: Why not? She helps ME make the beds!

✂

Uncle Joe bought his wife a canary, something she always wanted. The pet shop owner assured Joe that the canary sang beautifully. Joe brought the bird home and sure enough, it sang so sweetly that his wife was thrilled. On closer look, Joe was shocked to find the canary had only one leg. Angrily, he brought it back to the pet shop.

The owner said, "Well, what did you want? A singer or a dancer?"

✂

Uncle Joe was so clean he took a shower 3 times a day. When he died, in his memory, we ran the funeral procession through a car wash.

My aunt was very clean too. She hated a messy house. Uncle Joe said, "One night I got up at 2 a.m. to use-a the bathroom, and when I came-a back, my bed was made!

✂

Popular in the fifties was the Lawrence Welk Show, which advertised Geritol™ for tired blood.

Joe: Eh, To-nee. I'm-a real American. I watch Lawrence Welk and I take Geritol™.

Tony: Geritol™? Uncle Joe, that's for tired blood. You got tired blood?

Joe: I gonna **tell-a** you how tired. Last week I was shaving. I cutta myself. I no bleed until 3 days later. If that's-a not tired blood, I don't know what is!

✂

Uncle Nicola, to show off how smart he was, once took Uncle Joe to the museum:

Nicola: See this-a, Joe? This is what-a you call: "Egyptian mummy."

Joe: Egyptian's Mommy? He gotta Papa too?

Joe points to the dateline on the mummy: **49 B.C.** "What-sa this? His age?"

Nicola laughs: No, you greenhorn. That's-a license plate of the truck what-a kill-a him!

✂

Cousin Angelo came to America knowing no English at all. Uncle Joe taught him four words to order food in a restaurant. Angelo entered a diner, and said trembling, "Apple-a pie an' coffee." Without a word, the waitress filled his order. "It works!" marveled Angelo.

However, after a week of apple pie and coffee, he went back to Joe to learn something new. The next day Angelo went to the diner to try his new phrase, "Ham sandwich and coffee."

Waitress: May I help you?

Angelo: (slowly) Ham-a....sandwich-a....an' coffee.

Waitress: Yes, Sir. On white or on rye?

Angelo: (turning pale) Eh?

Waitress: I said, would you like that on white bread or rye bread?

Angelo: (throwing up his hands) Eh! Apple-a pie an' coffee!

✂

Luigi, a fruit peddler, wanted to be an American citizen. To all the judge's questions on American History, poor Luigi could answer only, "I dunno." The judge shook his head.

Luigi said, "Judge, now I ask **you** a question. How many bananas on a bunch?"

The judge answered, "I don't know."

Luigi smiled, "See, Judge? **You** know **your** business, and I know mine."

✂

Vincenzo and Luigi were best friends. Realizing that some day, one would die and leave the other behind, they made a pact: If reincarnation exists, whoever dies first will contact the other.

Luigi died first. Vincenzo grieved. One day, walking the neighborhood, he saw a sick, skinny horse, pulling a huge ice wagon. Then he heard a deep voice call "Vincenzo."

Vincenzo: That's-a Luigi's voice! Where are you, Luigi? I hear your voice, but I see just an old horse.

Luigi: This is my reincarnation. I'm a horse. I gotta cruel master. He beats me. He no give me enough food, and he make-a me pull this heavy ice wagon all day.

Vincenzo cried for his poor friend. Then he realized: "Luigi, you can talk! **Tell** your owner you need more food, and he can't treat you like this!"

Luigi: Shut up-a, Vincenzo. If that no good bum finds out I can talk, he'll have me yelling, "Ice! Ice!" all day long!

✂

An Italian lady went daily to St. Rocco's Church in Pittston to pray before the statue of the Blessed Mother for a good husband. One day, the sacristan, decided to have some fun.

The young woman knelt before the Blessed Mother in the empty church and repeated her plea, "Blessed Mother, please! Send me a good man!" From behind the Sacred Heart statue, a voice boomed, "NO!"

The woman jumped, looked around, then meekly said to the Sacred Heart, "I wasn't talkin' to you. I was-a talkin' to your Mother."

✂

An Italian mother-in-law came to visit for a week, but stayed two months. The daughter-in-law told her husband to send his mother home.

"I can't throw my mother out in cold blood!" the son said. "She hasn't done anything. If we had a fight or something, that would be different."

"Well," said the daughter-in-law, "then **START** a fight!" Tonight you say supper is terrible. I'll say it's good. We'll ask Mama. If she agrees with me, YOU throw her out. If she agrees with you, I'LL throw her out."

That night the son said his wife was a lousy cook and the food wasn't fit for pigs. The wife yelled that it was delicious, and he was an ungrateful bum. She then asked, "What do YOU think of this meal, Mama?"

Mama closed her eyes, shrugged her shoulders and said, I don't know nothing-a. I'm-a staying two more weeks!"

✂

A well-dressed man went to a fine Italian restaurant and asked for the best table in the house. After enjoying a 5-course meal and a bottle of imported wine, he called the owner. "Look, do whatever you want with me. Call the cops, beat me up, make me wash dishes, I don't care. You see, I have no money to pay for this meal."

The owner was angry, but then had an idea. "I'll make a deal with you," he said. "Across the street is another restaurant, run by my enemy. I hate him like poison. I'll forget about your bill, if tomorrow, you go over **there**, and do the same thing to **him**!"

"I can't do that," said the man. "I was over there yesterday, and **he** sent me over **here**!"

✂

Tony always told his family, "Never hold grudges. You hurt **yourself** when you refuse to forgive." He told this thought-provoking story, on how hatred harms **YOU** more than your enemy.

Antonio and Pasquale were bitter enemies. One day an angel told Pasquale that the Lord was displeased with their feud, and wanted Pasquale to **forgive**. As a reward, Pasquale would get ANYTHING he wished for, but Antonio would receive double.

Pasquale: You mean if I wish for a million dollars, I'll get it? But Antonio gets **two** million?

Angel: That's right.

Pasquale: And if I wish for a beautiful mansion Antonio gets **two** mansions?

Angel: Yes.

Pasquale: And if I get a gold Cadillac, **he** gets **two**?

Angel: (wearily) Yes, you'll get ANYTHING you wish for, and Antonio will get **two**.

Pasquale thought a while, then said viciously: "I wish for **ONE GLASS EYE!**"

✂ ✂ ✂ ✂ ✂

# TONY'S FAMOUS "PEANUTS and POPCORN" STORY

Luigi and Vincenzo went to the race track for the first time. They decided to study the names of all the horses until they found a name that "rang a bell."

Luigi shouted, "Look, Vincenzo, here's a horse named *Heels & Soles*. And I'm a shoemaker! Thats-a what-a you call a *hunch*. Like a sign. I'm-a gonna bet this-a one." Vincenzo agrees, and both go to place their bets. Lurking near the ticket window is a race-track "tout," one of those seedy-looking characters who hang around giving "inside tips."

Tout: Hey, Mister. Come here. Who you betting on?

Luigi: *Heels & Soles!* You see, I'm-a shoemaker, and that's a sign.

Tout: *Heels & Soles?* He can't win! Bet number seven. I know the owner, see. The favorite today is seven!

The smooth talker continued until Luigi and Vincenzo changed their bet.

Heels & Soles won, and number seven came in last. Luigi and Vincenzo were upset, but decided to try again. Vincenzo saw on the list a horse named *Pork Chop*. "Luigi," he shouted. "Look! I'm a butcher, and here's a horse, *Pork Chop*. That's a sign, no?" Luigi agrees, and they go to place their bets. There's the race track tout again.

Tales from the Barbershop

Tout: Hey, guys, listen, sorry about that last race. These things happen, see? But I have a hot tip on the next race. Number ten is definitely going to win.

Vincenzo: No! We're betting on *Pork Chop*. See, I'm-a butcher, and that's a sign.

Tout: Pork Chop? **He** can't win. Listen to me. I'm gonna let you in on a secret. (whispers) This race is fixed. Number ten is going to win. Bet number ten.

So Luigi and Vincenzo, afraid to defy the man's superior knowledge, bet number ten. You guessed it. *Pork Chop* wins, and number ten comes in last.

The two friends leave, angry and broke. "I got $2 for some peanuts," says Luigi. "Go to the refreshment stand, Vincenzo, and get 2 bags of peanuts, one for you and one for me."

Vincenzo comes back twenty minutes later, carrying two bags of **popcorn**!

Luigi: Whats-a matter with you, Vincenzo? I tell-a you go buy two bags of **peanuts**!

Vincenzo: (frustrated) Mama, mia, what could I do? I met that guy over at the stand again!!

✂ ✂ ✂ ✂ ✂

TONY'S CHURCH JOKES

Mike and Clancy were sitting on the steps of St. Patrick's as the Angelus began to ring:

Mike: Clancy, ain't the chimes beautiful?
Clancy: (shouting) What?
Mike: (shouting) I said, "Ain't the chimes beautiful?"
After the third time, Clancy yells: "It's no use—I can't hear a word you're saying with them damn bells ringing!

✂

A poor woman finally saved enough money to have a Mass said for her late husband.

Woman: Father, this is the first time I'm having a Mass said for my husband.
Priest: How long has he been dead?
Woman: 25 years.
Priest: (kindly) Keep your money, dear lady. By this time, he's either up or down.

✂

A man goes to confession. From his words and the liquor smell, Father realizes he's drunk.

Priest: My good man, you're drunk. Go home, sober up, and come back tomorrow.
Drunk: OK, Father.

Priest: (jokingly) Wait a minute—you didn't kill anyone did you?

Drunk: Oh, no, Father, I'd never kill anyone!

Priest: OK, then, come back tomorrow, son.

The man leaves, sees his friend on the church steps, and yells, "Hey, Joe, go home and come back tomorrow! He's only doing murder cases today."

✂

Parishoner: Please don't leave yet, Father. Join us for dinner. There's plenty of food.

Pastor: No, thanks. I'm preaching tonight, and I always speak better on an empty stomach.

After Mass, the pastor asked his parishoner, "Well, how did you like my sermon?"

The man answered, " Father...you might just as well have eaten."

✂

Another priest did stay for supper. Two fried chickens were served, and the hungry priest ate plenty. Suddenly the rooster out in the barn began to crow.

Priest: Listen to that rooster—how proudly he crows.

Farmer: Sure he's proud—he has 2 sons in the priesthood!

✂

Moe & Slug are sitting on the steps of St. Patrick's. Moe sees a sign, *"Confessions Today."*

Moe: I'm going to Confession!

Slug: Are you nuts? We ain't been to confession since we were kids!

Moe: I know. But I wanna turn over a new leaf.

Slug: OK….if **you** go, I will too.

They enter the empty church, blinking in the darkness after the bright sunshine. Stumbling into the confession box, Moe on one side, Slug on the other, Moe begins, "Bless me, Father, for I have sinned; it's 30 years since my last confession." And he tells all the sins of the past 30 years.

As Moe's eyes get used to the darkness, he sees there's no priest in the box. He can see his friend Slug across the confessional on the other side of the screen, listening.

Moe: Hey, Slug! Where's the priest?

Slug. I dunno…but if he heard what I heard, he's gone for the cops!

✂

Father X. was known for his **long** homilies. He came to Mass one day with Band-aids on his chin and said, "Sorry I'm late, folks. As I was shaving, I was concentrating on my sermon and I cut my chin."

After Mass a little old lady said, "Father, next time concentrate on your chin and cut your sermon!"

✂

Father noticed that one man in the first row fell asleep, week after week, during the homily. Father wanted to have a little fun, and **whispered** to the congregation: "All those who want to go to Heaven, stand up." Everyone stood, except Sleepy in the first row. Father whispered, "OK, now sit down."

He then shouted into the mike, "All those who want to go to Hell, STAND UP!"

The man awoke with a start, and stood all alone. Hearing laughter, he looked around, scratched his head, and said, "Father, I don't know what we're votin' for...but whatever it is, looks like you & me are the only two in favor of it."

✂

A young woman sitting up in the choir, leaned too far over the balcony and fell. Her skirt caught on the chandelier. She swayed back and forth in the air, undies showing. To spare her embarrassment, the minister shouted, "Any man who looks up, will be struck blind!"

One young fellow covered half his face and said, "I think I'll risk one eye."

✂

Priest baptizing baby: And what is the baby's name?

Godmother: Patrick Sean Michael Francis McGillicutty

Priest to altar boy: More holy water, please.

✂

A nun on her vow day had her gold band inscribed, "Lord, may I always be **thine**." Years later she lost weight. The ring was too big, so she had it cut a size smaller. Now the ring says, "Lord, may I always be **thin**."

✂

Three nuns went into a restaurant. Not recognizing their habit, the manager went over to ask them the name of their "order" of nuns. "Excuse me, Sisters, what's your order?"

They answered, "We'll have the lamb chops, please."

✂

Billy Graham, Pope John Paul, and Oral Roberts all die in the same plane crash. St. Peter is not prepared for their sudden arrival and has to get their mansions ready. He phones Lucifer: "Lucifer, I got three good men who belong in heaven, but I'm not ready for them. Can you put them up for a few days?" Lucifer reluctantly agrees.

The next day, Lucifer calls St. Peter: "Pete, get these guys out of here fast! They're ruining Hell. The Pope is going around **forgiving** everybody, Billy Graham is going around **saving** everybody, and Oral Roberts is raising money to have the place air conditioned!"

✂

Tony used to conclude his church jokes by thanking all the parishoners, "the pillars of the church," who had worked so hard for their parish.

"You know, in every parish, we have the pillars of the church, and the caterpillars.

The **pillars** hold up the church, and the **caterpillars** just run in and out."

✂ ✂ ✂ ✂ ✂

TONY'S SCHOOL JOKES

The local undertaker complained to Sr. Mary that her students were stealing signs from local stores and putting them on his funeral parlor door, embarrassing him.

"What do the signs say?" she asked.

"On Valentine's Day," said the mortician, "They stole a sign from the candy store that said, *TAKE HOME A BIG BOX FOR YOUR MOTHER IN LAW.*" And last week, they stole a THEATER sign that said, *"WE SELL BOX SEATS FOR TWO."*

Sister: Johnny, do you know how they make holy water?

Johnny: I think they boil the hell out of it.

✂

Sister: In the Our Father, why do we ask for DAILY bread. Why not ask enough for a week?

Joey: Because we want a fresh loaf every day.

✂

Sister heard a child swearing on the church steps. She told him how sad she was to hear a fine Christian boy using such words. The child solemnly promised to clean up his act.

Sister said, "Good for you, Son. You know, when I hear language like that, I get **cold chills** up and down my spine." The boy said, "Gee, Sister, good thing you wasn't at my house when my father hit his finger with the hammer——you'd-a **FROZE** to death!"

✂

A teacher rang the doorbell of her student's home.

Teacher: Tommy, I'd like to see your Mom and Dad, please.

Tommy: They was **in**, but they is **out** now.

Teacher: (imitating) "They was in, but they is out!" Tommy, where's your GRAMMAR?

Tommy: She's upstairs taking a nap.

✂

A little boy was being teased for crying on the playground.

"My dog died today," he whimpered.

The class bully sneered, "You big sissy—crying like that over a dog. My great grandmother died last week & I didn't cry at all."

"Yeah," sniffed the little boy, "but you didn't raise your great grandmother from a PUP!"

✂

Teacher: Name 5 things that contain milk.
Susie: Ice cream….butter…yogurt….and 2 cows!

✂

A kindergarten teacher asked the son of a gambler, how high he could count.

The little boy answered, "1-2-3-4-5-6-7-8-9-10-Jack-Queen-King."

✂

The Bishop at Confirmation asked, "What is Matrimony?"

One boy nervously rattled off, "Matrimony is a place of temporary punishment, where good people must suffer for a time, before they can enter the kingdom of heaven."

The pastor was embarrassed and said, "Here, son, you're confused. You gave the definition of **PURGATORY**."

The Bishop said, "Leave the boy alone, Father, maybe he has a point there. Besides, what do you & I know about it anyway?"

✂

Teacher: Class, these plants begin with the word DOG. This is called a DOG ROSE. Here's a DOG-VIOLET, and this tree is a DOGWOOD. Can you name any more?

Class Clown: Collie-flower

Teacher: How can you always tell a dogwood tree?

Class Clown: By its bark!

Teacher: What did Julius Caesar say when Brutus stabbed him?

Class clown: Ouch!

✂

The teacher was fed up with the class clown. The last straw occurred one day:

Teacher: Who was responsible for the Magna Carta?

Class Clown: Don't look at me-**I didn't do it!**

At PTA, Sister told the clown's parents about the fresh Magna Carta answer.

The father protested, "Sister, I know my kid's no angel, but just once, couldn't you believe him? If he says he didn't do it, maybe he REALLY didn't do it.

The mother turned on the father, "See! **That's** why our son is the way he is. You always defend him! Sister, don't worry. I know that kid. He did it! When I get home, I'll fix him good and he'll never do it again!"

✂

Teacher: Judy, are you chewing gum or eating candy?

Judy No, Ma'am.

Teacher: Then what's that big **lump** in your cheek?

Judy: I'm just soaking a prune to eat at recess.

Next day the same little girl had a lump in her cheek.

Teacher: (holding out her hand) Come here and give me whatever you have in your mouth.

Judy: I wish I could. It's a toothache.

✂

Jakie, a little Jewish boy, asked Mother Superior, "How am I doing in this school?

Sister said, "Jakie, you're doing fine. Just correct 3 things:

1st Don't hang your hat on the crucifix.
2nd Don't wash your face in the holy water, and
3rd Stop calling me Mother **Shapiro**."

✂

The kindergarten class was going to entertain the PTA: Five tots would run out on stage each holding a card with one letter of H-E-L-L-O. The last child was so nervous that he fell with his **O**, leaving that 4-letter word to greet the PTA. His teacher, down in the orchestra pit said, "Johnny, that's OK. Pick up your O and run to the end of the line."

Johnny got up, but in his confusion, he ran with his O to the BEGINNING of the line!

✂

Tony liked to tell this story at Mother's Day Banquets:

During the school play, a little girl had to recite a Bible verse, beginning with, "I am the Light of the World."

She stood on stage and went blank.

Her mother crept to the footlights and whispered, "Honey, say: 'I am the Light of the World.' "

The little girl shouted, "My mother is the Light of the World."

Tony ended: "What insight that child had! Aren't our good mothers the Light of the World?"

✂ ✂ ✂ ✂ ✂

MISCELLANEOUS JOKES

A man taking a trip asked his brother to care for his beloved cat. After a week, he phoned:

Man: How's my cat?

Brother: Oh, it died.

Man: What? You cruel man! How could you break the news to me just like that?

Brother: Well, how was I **supposed** to tell you?

Man: You don't shock a person with bad news! You say it gradually! You could have said... like... "Well, you see, the cat climbed up on the roof. We couldn't get him down...and he fell...and we called the vet. But the vet couldn't save him and he died." This way, the person is prepared for the bad news at the end.

Brother: I'm sorry. I didn't know that. I'll know from now on. Forgive me.

Man: All right. I forgive you. Now how's Mama?

Brother: Uh...Well...you see...she climbed up on the roof.......

✂

Mr. Moscowitz was playing cards one night, lost $500, had a heart attack and died. His buddies chose Sam to go home and tell the wife, but warned him to break it to her gently:

Sam: Mrs. Moscowitz, I have some bad news. Your husband was playing cards and he lost $500.

Wife: $500 he lost? That bum! He should drop dead!

Sam: He did!

✂

A jet plane was flying over Italy:

Pilot: Ladies and Gentlemen, we are now flying over the beautiful Bay of Naples. Have any of you ever heard the saying, "See Naples and die?"

Flyer: Yes, I've heard that saying!

Pilot: Well, take a good look. Our propeller just fell off!

✂

Judge: State your name, your occupation, and what you're charged with.

Criminal: My name is Sparks, I'm an electrician, and I'm charged with battery.

Judge: Put this guy in a dry cell.

✂

Joe could no longer stand his wife's nagging, so he built himself a little log cabin in the back yard. Each day when he returned from work, his wife would bring his paper and hot supper on a tray. They would chat for a while; then she would return to her house.

A friend said, "Hey, Joe, you have it nice. She brings your meals, your paper...she's so good to you."

"Yeah," admitted Joe. "I couldn't live under the same roof with that woman, but she sure makes a wonderful neighbor!

✂

A husband and wife were married for 60 years. The local reporter came for an interview and asked the husband, "In all those years, did you ever consider divorce?

"DIVORCE? NEVER!" was the answer. "**Murder**, yes...but divorce NEVER."

✂

A 50-year-old man and his 50-year-old wife were marooned on an island. A genie appeared, offering them one wish each.

The wife said, "I wish I were back home in my own little house." And **poof**! She **was**!

The husband then made his wish: "I want a wife 30 years younger than I am!" And **poof**! He was 80 years old!

✂

A man went to heaven and was shocked to see he was the only one there.

Yes," said God, "The world is so bad, you're the first one who ever made it up here."

At supper, God brought out two cheese sandwiches. Looking down, the man could see Hell—flames, screams, and torment, but everyone was sitting at a **long** table, at a 5-course banquet.

"Lord," protested the man, "they're in Hell having a banquet, and I'm in heaven with just a cheese sandwich?"

God answered, "Hey, I'm not gonna cook for just two people."

✂

A freeloader dropped in unexpectedly on friends at dinner time. Later he described the meal.

"They invited me to sit down and join them, and I never saw such bad manners in all my life! We were seven people, and they had only seven pork chops on the platter. (pause) But the two I had were good!"

✂

A Florida real estate man was trying to make a sale. "Our climate here is so healthful—nobody ever dies!" Just then a funeral procession passed by. The real estate man sighed and said, "Poor old undertaker. He starved to death."

✂

Joe loved golf more than anything else! One day during a crucial swing on the golf course, he saw a funeral procession passing on the highway. He stopped, placed his golf cap over his heart, and said a prayer. Then he continued playing.

The caddy said, "Sir, that was very nice. You love golf so much, yet you stopped to pray for the dead."

Joe nodded sadly. "Yes, she was a wonderful woman. We would have been married 30 years next week."

✂

Husband: I haven't spoken to my wife in two years.

Friend: How come?

Husband: I didn't want to interrupt her.

✂

A heartbroken widower engraved on his dead wife's tombstone these words: **The Light of My Life Has Gone Out.**

Friends watched as the husband knelt at the grave and wept. "He'll never get over it," they whispered sadly.

A month later, the man remarried. He was a little embarassed about the message on the tombstone. So he added a line: **But I Struck Another Match.**

✂

A man was kneeling at a stone monument in a cemetary, sobbing, "Why did you have to **die**? **Why** did you have to die?"

A woman approached and said kindly, "I'm so sorry for your troubles, my good man. **Who** is buried here?

The man sobbed, "My wife's first husband."

✂

A tenant and his landlady were always fighting.

Landlady: If you were my husband, I'd give you poison!

Tenant: If you were my wife, I'd **take** it!

✂

A rich man wanted to send his mom a special Mother's Day gift! He went into a pet shop and saw a parrot that cost $10,000.

Man: Why is this parrot so expensive?

Owner: Mister, that bird can speak **seven languages**?

Man: Wow, just the gift for my mother! Here's her address. Send it right away.

A week later, the man called his mother.

Man: Mama, how did you like the bird I sent you for Mother's Day?

Mama: Oh, thank you, Son, I **loved** it! It was **delicious**, and so **tender**!"

Man: What!!?? You **ate** that parrot? Mama, how could you? That bird cost me $10,000! He could speak seven languages!

Mama: Well, then . . . why didn't he **say** something?

✂

A reporter treated his priest friend to a ticket to a boxing match. As the bell rang, one of the fighters made the sign of the cross. The reporter asked the priest, "Father, does that help him?" The priest answered, "It **does**--if he can **fight**."

✂

A man at the race track saw a priest making the sign of the cross over a horse, which was lying down in the stable. The man thought, "That horse is sure to win," and he bet a week's salary on the horse.

The horse came in last. The man was devastated. Leaving the race track, he saw the priest. "Hey, Father!" he shouted. "I lost a lot of money today because of you! I saw you kneeling over that horse, giving him a special blessing to win!"

The priest smilled kindly. "I'm sorry, my good man. You misunderstood. I wasn't giving that horse a blessing to win. I was giving him the Last Rites!"

An old maid was reading an article in the newspaper about a woman who had just cremated her third husband. "Hmph!" snorted the spinster. "It's not fair! I can't get **one** husband, and she has husbands to burn!"

Jim was an atheist. He died and was laid out in a beautiful new suit. His friend stood near the coffin and said, "Poor Jim. He didn't believe in Heaven and he didn't believe in Hell. He's all dressed up, and he has no place to go."

Girl: Mother, John asked me to marry him . . . but he doesn't believe in Hell!

Mother: Marry him, Dear. Between the two of us, we'll soon convince him there's a Hell!

MAKE FUN OF YOURSELF, NOT OTHERS

Tony often said, "A good comedian makes fun of himself, not others." He never joked about other people's physical defects, but would joke about his own bald head. Here he tells what a flop he was at his last speaking engagement.

Boy, I'm glad to be with you people at today's banquet! Nobody clapped for me yesterday!

First I went to the mental hospital. The doctor said, "Tell the patients some jokes to cheer them up, but **don't** take anything personally."

As I entered the big hall, a man in the front row glared angrily at me. The doctor said, "That poor man always looks that way. He hasn't spoken nor shown any sign of awareness for ten years." So I told my first joke. The angry man in the first row yelled, "Rotten!" I looked at the doctor. He whispered, "Keep talking."

I told my second joke and the man yelled again, "Rotten!" Doctor patted my arm: "Keep talking."

When the man yelled, "Rotten!" after my **third** joke, I asked, "Doctor, shall I stop?"

"No, no!" protested the doctor. "You're doing a world of good! That's the first sign of intelligence that man has shown in **ten** years!"

L ater a patient came up to me and said, "You're the **worst** speaker we ever had here!"

The nurse said kindly, "Oh, don't pay attention to her. She doesn't know what she's saying. She just goes around repeating what she hears **everyone else** saying!"

Another patient told me, "You're the best speaker we ever had! You're not like those **others** they send here. **You're** more like one of **us**!

✂

Then the doctor gave me a tour. One man was walking up and down the halls crying, "Rosie....Ro-o-sie...." The doctor said, "He's harmless. His girl left him to marry his best friend. He just walks up and down all day crying for Rosie." Then we came to the padded cells where the violent were kept. One man kept banging his head against the wall, shouting and cursing. The doctor said, "That's the guy that **married** Rosie."

✂

Then we toured the garden. A nurse had three patients out for some fresh air. Just then a farmer passed the gate with a wagon of horse manure.

"Where are you going with that foul-smelling stuff?' asked one patient.

The farmer said, "I'm going to put it on my strawberries."

The patient shook his head sadly, "And they say **we're** crazy! **We** put **cream** on **our** strawberries!"

✂

I also had a rough time when I went to tell jokes at the prison:

I began, "My good men!" And the prisoners snickered sarcastically because I said *good* men.

I tried again: "My fellow *citizens*!" And they mocked me again. You see, in prison, you temporarily lose your citizenship privileges: the right to vote, and so on.

So I covered up my embarrassment by laughing and saying, "Well, **anyway**! I'm glad to see so many of you **here**!"

Which is why I love to come to **your** banquet here at St. Rocco's. Here I can say, "My good people, or my fellow citizens, and I can safely say, **"I'm happy to see so many of you here!"**

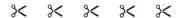

TONY'S "HAIR-RAISING" MIRACLE

Every April, Pittston's *Sunday Dispatch*, used to run a "spoof" section, "Looking at Life through April Fool Glasses." Everyone knew the stories were not true and had a good laugh.

One year the *Dispatch* ran **two** pictures of my Dad, **BEFORE** and **AFTER**. The **BEFORE** photo showed Tony as he was, a handsome, prematurely bald man in his forties. **AFTER** was the same photo, on which the *Dispatch* had "added" a head of thick, wavy hair.

I wish I had the original article to reproduce here! Since I don't, here's my own paraphrase as I recall it, decades later.

The article said that Tony had gone to the barber shop to try a new brand of floor wax on his linoleum floor. Before leaving the shop, he rubbed some hair tonic on the few hairs behind his ears, and across his entire bald scalp.

As he headed briskly for the door, he slipped and fell on his head, sliding several feet across the newly-waxed floor. He then rubbed liniment on his head bruises, and went home to bed. The next morning, he was shocked to find that he had a full head of dark, wavy curls.

Examining doctors agreed that the combined chemicals in the hair tonic, floor wax, and liniment, plus the friction incurred by sliding across the floor on his head, had caused Tony's miraculous hair growth. Tony has bottled the mixture for sale. Customers will receive free band-aids for bruises caused by sliding across the floor on their heads during the friction aspect of the hair restorer. So ran the April Fool story.

Pittston laughed, and Tony loved it! The story traveled far, and got distorted in the retelling. We got a phone call from Texas, asking to buy the hair restorer they had heard about from the friend of a friend. This created another *Dispatch* column — a follow-up of the "miraculous" April Fool story.

✂

How did the *Dispatch* invent the April Fool Story? Here's my theory. When I was twelve, my Dad trimmed six inches off my long hair. Gathering the cut locks from our kitchen floor, he placed them into a hair net, which he plopped on his head. He and I then walked up and down James and Market Streets to the neighbors sitting on their front porches (the days before TV).

Daddy told them he had prayed for a miracle, and his hair had grown overnight. Neighbors howled as he moved from porch to porch with his "hair." Then he walked over to John Street, to Frank and Lina Rostock's Grocery Store, shouting in Italian "*Miracolo!*" (Miracle!) I remember gazing at Mrs. Rostock, fascinated by her long, loud cackle.

Daddy was pleased that he had made so many people laugh. I think neighbors told our friends Billy Watson, *Dispatch* Editor, and Dick Cosgrove, *Dispatch* columnist, and they did the rest.

✂ ✂ ✂ ✂ ✂

Young, handsome Tony, on Pittston's "New Bridge" over the Susquehanna River. "The catch of 1935," his proud bride often said.

Tony with wife, Josephine Manganaro Palmeri, and author, baby Josie, named after Tony's Mom. Three siblings named daughters for Nanna Josephine in that era, unwritten law in Italian-American families.

Tony and young brother, Buster, buddies and business partners for 40 years.

Out for some sidewalk philosophy with passerby.

There was no little boy whom Tony could not charm into having a haircut.

A quiet moment in the shop.

Tony cuts the hair of close friend Charlie Maria.

Tales From The Barbershop

The foursome: Tony and Jo, with daughters Josie and young Santina

Tony with his Mom, daughter Santina Palmeri Lonergan, with grandchildren, Lynn and Brian, which Nanna pronounced Lina and Bruni. Baby Christopher Anthony would arrive later.

Tony's Dad, Luigi Palmeri, from Serra di Falco, Sicily. He was called "Barbarossa" for his reddish hair and mustache.

Tony & Jo's Silver Wedding Anniversary with Santina, Sister Josephine, M.P.F., and Nanna Josephine, center.

Nanna Josephine on her 100th birthday with Father Julio Serra, O.S.J., pastor of St. Rocco's Church, Pittston. Nanna would live to be 104 with good health, good memory, and no eyeglasses.

Villa Walsh Convent in Morristown, New Jersey, on visiting day.

Tales From The Barbershop   53

The February 12, 1978, issue of the "Sunday Dispatch" highlighted Tony and his 'kid brother Buster' for their long careers as barbers, and for Tony's fame as a humorist.

Tony can't talk without using his hands.

Entertaining at the Treadway Inn

Tony's calling card, simple and direct--like the man himself.

A younger Tony in a news clip, one of hundreds.

Tony in his 60's, a few years before his death. Even in his last illness, the gentle hazel eyes and friendly smile won hearts.

Tales From The Barbershop

HOW TONY SAVED THE DROWNING DOG

My Dad was afraid of big dogs, and his two daughters inherited his fear. Tony loved people, but for some reason, he was not an animal lover. Except for Rex, the little family dog he had known as a boy, both he and my mother preferred not to have four-legged critters in the house.

Arriving at a nursing home to shave a bedridden customer one day, Tony saw two huge watch dogs, "the size of Shetland ponies," he recalled, running down the hill toward him. He leaped back into his car and locked the door. Out came a tiny nun who grabbed the two dogs by the collar, scolded them, and said, "That's OK, Mr. Palmeri, you can come out now. I've got them."

Tony opened the window a crack. "Please, Sister, before I get out, put the dogs inside. I read once that when you're afraid of dogs, you give off a chemical odor that makes a dog attack you. Sister, right now, I'm giving off so much chemical odor, that **they'll eat the two of us!**" The nun laughed, put the dogs inside, and Tony's customer got his haircut and shave.

However, decades before, our Pittston paper ran a story about how the young barber had put aside his fears to save a drowning dog. The yellow clipping which I had read and reread as a child has been lost, but here is my memory of it:

Young Tony, dressed in his best Sunday suit, needed to get something from his barber shop after early Mass. Suddenly he heard a pitiful whimper coming from a nearby catch basin, an opening in the gutter for catching rain water, which was quite high after Saturday night's storm. Kneeling down in the wet gutter, Tony peered in to see a dog in the catch basin, crying and desperately paddling to stay afloat in the swollen waters. In spite of his fear of a dog bite, Tony felt pity for the frightened animal and thrust his arms in to see if he could reach him. No luck.

Just then a paper boy on a bike came along, his newspapers tied together with a rope. Tony borrowed the rope, tied it into a loop, and lowered it into the catch basin. The dog clenched the rope with his teeth, and Tony was able to pull him out.

The dog followed Tony to the shop, where my father took him in and rubbed him dry and warm with an old terry cloth towel.

Now the pooch was in love with Tony, followed him out of the shop, around town, close to his heels. As good luck would have it, my Dad met the same paper boy again and paid him to tie the rope to the dog's collar and detain him for a few minutes until he could get out of sight.

A local reporter just happened to be around, and the dog–in-the-catch-basin story became another Pittston favorite.

TODAY'S SPOILED KIDS

Tony loved kids, but enjoyed contrasting the indulgent parents of today with his own tough upbringing. Here's his famous monologue:

Nowadays you have to beg kids to eat. I heard a mother say, "Please eat, Honey, and I'll give you a dollar." The kid said, "**Two** dollars, and 2 comic books and it's a deal!"

In my day, if you took your eye off your plate, somebody stole your potato!

Once my parents saved up all week for a nice chicken dinner. After Sunday Mass we could smell chicken roasting, and the homemade apple pies my mother baked. Right at dinner time, in walks my Uncle Joe with his five kids.

My mother called us into the parlor. "Children, listen." she said. "We have company and there's not enough food to go around. I must make a good showing in front of Uncle Joe. So don't take any chicken. I'll coax you and pretend to be mad, but **don't** take any food. Say you're not hungry. I'll make it up to you another time."   Sigh. We had to obey.

At the table, we had to lie, "Ma, I'm not hungry." My mother insisted, "Take some! Eat!" More lies, "No, Ma, honest, we're not hungry."

Meanwhile, we watched our uncle and our cousins devour our chicken. But, we knew—there were those delicious apple pies on the stove.

"Ah, but I'll never forgive my mother for what she did next. Serving those hot pies, she announced, "Now, all those who wouldn't eat their chicken....don't get no apple pie!"

Yes, the kids of today are spoiled. **We** obeyed or got hit. Nowadays, a mother reads her child psychology book. She looks up *What to Do When Johnny Kicks Mommy in the Shins.*

The chapter says, "This is an expression of Johnny's free spirit. To stop him would frustrate his freedom. Until he outgrows this stage, Mommy should wear shin guards."
    I know one family whose son was so spoiled he became incorrigible. Denying him anything made him scream until he turned blue. They took him to a child psychologist who said, "This boy has had his own way so long, that it's too late to change him. He'll get frustrated and sick. Don't worry, he'll outgrow it in time. For now, give him everything he asks for."
    The poor parents paid the doctor and went home. The next meal went something like this:

Mommy: Eat, Sweetheart. Look at the lovely dinner we have.
Johnny: I won't eat it.
Mommy: Why not, honey?
Johnny: I don't like what we're having.
Mommy: Well, what would you like?
Johnny: I want to eat a worm.

Both parents shudder, plead, but Johnny insists.

Mom: Please, Dear, remember what the doctor said. Go out in the yard and find him a worm.

Daddy comes back with a worm, rinses it off, and puts it on the child's plate.

Johnny: I don't want it like that. I want Daddy to BOIL it!

Mom gazes pleadingly at Dad, who boils the worm and puts it on the dish.

Johnny: I won't eat it—unless Daddy eats half—FIRST!

Daddy: Now, wait a minute! Enough is enough! HE's the one who wants the worm! I dug it, I boiled it, but I'll be damned if I'll eat it.

(Johnny screams, bangs feet, turns blue.)

Mom: Darling, please, he's our only son. Remember what the doctor said.

Daddy gulps, cuts the worm in two, covers half with ketchup, closes his eyes…and swallows.

Johnny: (screams) No! No! No! I won't eat it!

Mommy: What's wrong **now**, Sweetheart?

Johnny: (screams) Daddy ate the half that I wanted!

Tony concluded: "At this point, the parents forgot the doctor and the child psychology book, and gave the kid a good spanking."

✂ ✂ ✂ ✂ ✂

TONY'S MAGIC

"Inside of every old woman is a beautiful young girl," Tony used to say.

I didn't realize how sick my Dad was that day he drove me to visit my friend at Laurel Hill Nursing Home in Dunmore, Pennsylvania. "Let's not stay long," he said. "I feel dizzy."

Dad met 82-year-old May, with her blue eyes and dyed red hair. He shook her hand and said charmingly, "May, I bet I can guess two things about you. With that lovely face, you must be **Irish**." "Yes!" May marveled.

And second, if you're this pretty now, at age 17 you must have been a **beauty**!"

May's eyes brimmed over with tears. "Tony, I hate to brag, but I <u>was</u>!"

As we left, Dad asked if he could give her a hug. May smiled, "Tony, I'd be honored."

On my next visit, before even greeting me, May demanded, "Where's your father?" When I told her he had died, she cried.

"What kind of man can make this impact on another human being in one five-minute visit?" I wondered.

People had different names for Tony's gift: *charisma, charm, joy*! Others called it ***Magic***!

✂ ✂ ✂ ✂ ✂

As a little girl, I loved to have my bangs trimmed in my Daddy's shop. It was fun to play with the shaving cream machine, sit up high on the shoe shine stand, and read the comic books. Tony also had a candy counter, but refused to sell anything stale. He gave all unsold candy free to neighborhood children each weekend, and put out a fresh supply on Monday morning. I wrote this poem years later as a college writing assignment.

TONSORIAL TREATS

A Child's Impression

In Tony's place, the shaving cream spurts out of
a shiny black box
like wiggly, white snakes.
You press the button; fluff piles up like marshmallow clouds
right there in your hand.

Shoeshine rags go ziggety-zag. You climb up high to have
your shoes shined with a big, brown brush.
Cold steel scissors snippety-snip;
the humming clippers tickle your neck.
But you don't mind.

Tony says if you watch the sheet that covers you
like a blue-striped tent,
a bunny peeks out.

Miles of mirrors panel the walls; gleaming bottles
on long glass shelves
sparkle and shine.
Little hair piles dot the black-&-white floor;
Tony goes for a big long broom
to sweep them all up.

Tony's white coat smells of lotion & talc. If you sit still in
the spin-around chair,
he'll talcum you and spin you around.

Then Mother comes to take you home, but Tony first
will give you a gift:
a comic book, and a package of Charms
and he shakes your hand,
and calls you a champ.

✂ ✂ ✂ ✂ ✂

Tales from the Barbershop

THE ORPHANS' HAIRCUTS

Tony loved to go to St. Stanlislaus Orphanage in Sheatown, PA, to donate his service cutting the hair of the orphans. He was joined by other Pittston barbers who gave this labor of love each time the nuns requested it.

One day, due to a mix-up, only two barbers showed up, Tony and friend, Sam Amico. With 72 boys needing summer crew cuts, Sam and Tony would have to cut hair eight hours straight.

One of the nuns said, "Teach me to cut, and I'll help you." She was a fast learner, and soon mastered the clippers, doing the preliminary work, while Tony and Sam kept cutting and trimming the long line of little boys. After standing for four hours and cutting non-stop, the tired barbers could barely keep their arms raised.

The Bible tells of a battle between the Israelites and their enemies. As Moses, watching from a hill, kept his arms upraised in prayer, the Israelites kept winning. When Moses' arms dropped in exhaustion, the Israelites began to lose. So two fellow-Israelites, one on each side of Moses, held his arms aloft. The prayers continued, and the Chosen People won the battle.

Perhaps inspired by this story, Sister announced to the children, "Everybody pray out loud for God to give the barbers strength to finish their work!" The little boys began to recite the Rosary in unison. Tony and Sam were deeply moved by the young voices chanting their chorus of prayers, and the haircuts were completed that day.

The *Dispatch* heard the story, and the two barbers, who had gone to work quietly for the Lord, became heroes.

✂ ✂ ✂ ✂ ✂

WISDOM AND BRAINS BUT NO DIPLOMA

Tony knew the value of education, but he admired unschooled people with wisdom and common sense. "They don't always come with a diploma," he'd say. Though a native-born American, Dad liked to quote the wisdom found in old Italian proverbs.

After a simple-but-nourishing meal in the peace and tranquility of his home, Dad liked to say, "*Ah, meglio pane e cipuddi con amore....*" the first half of the saying, "Better to eat bread and onions with love....than a banquet with strife." Years later I found in the Bible: "Better to eat a dish of herbs in peace, than a fatted calf with strife and hatred." (Proverbs 15:17) With no theology courses, our immigrant ancestors had wisdom direct from the Holy Spirit.

"*Chi sputa nell'aria, ti ritorna alla faccia.*" (If you spit in the air—it lands in your face.) Tevye the Jewish milkman quoted this in "Fiddler on the Roof," so it must be a proverb known to many ethnic groups. However, I heard it at home years before Tevye said it on Broadway. Our good Irish neighbors used to say, "Chickens come home to roost—what goes around, comes around." The Bible sums it up: "What you sow, you shall reap." (Galatians 6:7)

"*Meglio solo, que mal accompagnato.*" (Better to be alone than with bad companions.)

"*Non cercare il pelo nel'ova.*" (Don't look for a hair on the egg.) Said to people who try to find fault where none exists.

"*Fa bene e scordalo; fa male e ricordalo.*" (Do good and forget. Do evil and remember.) Don't seek reward for your good deeds, but remember your mistakes so you won't repeat them.

Hard work was a virtue. "*Chi dorme non piglia pesci.*" (He who sleeps catches no fish.)

Prudent speech was extolled: "*La parola chiu meglia é chidda che non si dice.*" (Sicilian dialect for "The best word is the one you don't say." or "The less said, the better.") "*Pensi lu malu, che ti vene lu bonu.*" Literally, "Think of the bad, then good will come to you." Before doing wrong, think of the bad consequences. Then you won't do wrong, and you'll have peace of mind.

"Never steal, Honey," Dad continued. If you want something, tell me, and I'll buy it for you." Concerned for the virtue of his daughters, he urged at a tender age, "If anyone says, 'Come with me and I'll give you a bracelet,' you say, 'No, thank you. My father will buy it for me.' Then tell Daddy, and I'll buy you the bracelet." He was always true to his word. I once asked for a dime (which went far in the 1940's) for a Woolworth trinket. "No!" he said with a twinkle in his eye, "You must take a **quarter**!" My sister Santina and I were not tempted by material things, knowing they were ours for the asking. And since we grew up in a little coal mining town, where others had less than we did, we never asked for too much.

"*Chi male fa, male aspetta.*" (Evil awaits those who do evil.)

Friends of ours were taught to thank God, "*con faccia per terra e culo nell'aria.*" (with your face to the ground, and tush in the air.) Logical—that's where your tush goes when you kiss the ground in gratitude.

Although not a millionaire, Tony was wise enough to realize how rich he was in every other way. We once read a news article about a shabby old man in a diner, whose waitress felt sorry for him and went out of her way to smile and give him the royal treatment. He turned out to be an eccentric rich man, who left her a million dollars in gratitude for "her million-dollar smile."

"How come that never happened to you, Daddy?" we asked. "You're kind to everyone, and you always go out of your way for people. How come **you** never got a million dollars?"

"I did," he said. "Look around this dinner table. The four of us have **never** been in the hospital, have never even been **sick**. *That's* worth a million dollars!"

Daddy worked hard in his barber shop, and Mom was a good manager, who could stretch a dollar. A one-woman man who loved his wife, he took us all to church on Sunday, then out for pancakes, and back home to enjoy the newspapers, as tomato sauce simmered on the stove. After dinner, we all walked to the American theater for the Sunday movie. The aroma of fresh popcorn—a big box for five cents—was part of the ritual. And after the movies, to Russell's Ice Cream Parlor, where they served two dips for a nickel. I always thought we were rich!

Tony never envied people with great material wealth. "May they enjoy it in good health," was his motto. Once, a former friend, who had grown up in the same humble neighborhood as Tony, was trying to flaunt his new-found wealth.

Friend: See this watch, Tony? I paid 200 bucks for it!

Tony: See this Timex? Ten bucks. What time does your $200 watch say?

Friend: Four o'clock.

Tony: Wow! My Timex says 4:00 too! So you paid $200 to know the time, and I can find out for ten!

Friend: Aw, come on, Tony. Admit you're impressed. I got $50 ties, I got luxury cars. You name one thing I don't got.

Tony laughed, "Jim, you don't got good manners!"

My father admired education and was proud that his daughters were teachers with Master's degrees. But he often warned us: "Never look down on those with no diploma; they may have goodness and wisdom beyond book knowledge. Look at your Mother—she has more common sense in her little finger than you two girls put together—no offense." And we knew he was right.

When my sister had her first child, she phoned my mother frantically one day. "I just gave the baby his bottle and he's screaming, and I can't make him stop!" My mother replied calmly, "Honey, just hold him over your shoulder, and pat his back. He may have a bit of gas pain. He'll be OK." A few minutes later, Santina called back, "Mommy, I did what you said, and he let out a big burp and fell asleep. How did you know what was wrong?" Dad grabbed the phone, deliberately using bad English to sound like Archie Bunker. "That's easy! She knows because she don't have no Master's Degree! Both you and your sister the nun—the more you study, the less common sense you have. Remember, Santina, there's nothing as ignorant as an educated man when you take him off the subject he was educated in. Now, if we take you off the subject of history—what do you know? Take your sister the nun off the topic of Spanish—what does she know? Nothing. Your mother has more common sense than you two kids put together."

We all laughed. And then we heard for the umpteenth time his favorite sayings:

"It's **nice** to be **important**, but it's more **important** to be **nice**."
"Be good to the little people on your way to the top, because you're going to meet them again on the way down."

And as usual, he was right!

✂ ✂ ✂ ✂ ✂

"WASTING TIME" with GOD

My Dad spiced every meal with jokes, stories, philosophy, poetry. We didn't realize then how his words were shaping our lives, or how my Grandpa had shaped his. Here's my favorite story:

As a child, Tony loved to walk with his father, Luigi, to Sunday Mass at St. Rocco's Church. Luigi, who had worked all week in the dark, damp coal mines, found comfort in his Catholic faith and in the beauty of his parish church, with its statues, glowing candles, and decorated altars.

On the way, they had to pass the Italian Men's Club. The non-churchgoers among them liked to tease Luigi. One day, the exchange (in Italian, of course) went like this:

Friend: Eh, Luigi, where you go?

Luigi: To Mass.

Friend: (laughter) Well, you say a Hail Mary for us.

Luigi: Better come and say your own Hail Mary. I might forget.

Friend: Luigi, you waste your time. **Non c'e niente lassú.** (There's nothing up there.)

Luigi waved goodbye and walked on to Mass, holding his little son's hand. Tony was upset. How could those men say there was "nothing up there?" He was taught at home that **Heaven** was there, **God** was there, and everywhere else too. "Papa," he asked in alarm, "Why did they say church is a waste of time? Is it true there's nothing up there?"

Luigi answered calmly, "Well, *figlio mio* (my son), here's how I see it. *If* there's nothing up there, I don't waste time going for a walk with my boy in the nice sunshine. We see the beautiful church, we sing the songs, say the prayers, hear the choir and the nice music. We hear the priest, educated man, give us a talk. That's not wasting time. But if there *is* something up there," he added with a knowing wink, "it's gonna be there, waiting for us."

✂ ✂ ✂ ✂ ✂

NANNA'S SUBWAY MIRACLE

Tony's character was formed by his hard-working immigrant parents. Though unschooled, they had common sense, wisdom, and solid spirituality.

Tony's father, Luigi, often reminded his son of the Sicilian proverb, "*Pensi lu malu che ti vene lu bonu,*" or, "Think of the bad, then good will come to you." In other words, before doing wrong, think of the bad consequences, and you won't do it. Then good things will come to you: a clear conscience with a peaceful night's sleep, and the greatest gift of all, a good name, worth more than riches.

As a child, Tony once took a bag of peanuts from the five-and-dime store. He proudly showed Luigi, "Look, Papa, and I didn't even have to pay for it because the lady didn't see me take it. " Luigi was furious. He marched his little son back to the store and demanded, "You give back to the lady, and you tell her you're sorry." Tony was humiliated, but admitted proudly "And I never stole anything again in my whole life."
Modern psychology might say that Luigi gave his child a traumatic experience which would scar him for life. Tony disagreed.

Just as strong in the character-building department was Tony's mom, Josephine Giarratano Palmeri. We called her Nanna or simply Nah. She was tough. She had to be. When she was a child in Siciliy, the people in her little village of Serra di Falco almost died during a famine when the crops failed. How Josephine cried when her pet rooster, Ferlino, had to be killed for food. Her family calculated that if they ate only every other day, the sacks of flour, beans, and other staples would last through the winter. One day, she woke up under the kitchen table. She had fainted, but her family did not revive her.

"While she's unconscious, she won't know how hungry she is," her mother said. "Put her under the table with a pillow under her head, safe from harm."

Years later she came to America with husband Luigi, and toddlers Jenny and Theresa. They settled in the Wyoming Valley area of Pittston, Pennsylvania, where the only job Luigi could find was in the anthracite coal mines. Three more children joined the family: Tony, Sebastian (Buster), and Providenza (Pru).

Miner's asthma, also known as "Black Lung" made it impossible for Luigi to continue in the coal mines, so he began his own business. Buying two horses, Nellie and Sport, plus a big wagon, he became a rag man and scrap metal collector, earning enough to feed five kids and buy his own home during the Depression, without going on welfare or "relief" as they called it back then. "No work is beneath our dignity, as long as it's *honest* work," Tony's parents believed.

Nanna took her two teenage boys to a local barber, Johnny Martin. "Teach them your trade, please," she begged. "They will work hard for you for no pay. I don't want my sons to die in the mines."

Tony loved to tell how Babe Ruth stopped in the shop one day. A teenaged apprentice barber could not shave the great ball player, of course, but Tony begged Johnny Martin for the privilege of lathering him up. Kind Mr. Martin agreed. Tony was so nervous that he got a bit of soap in Babe Ruth's mouth, and apologized profusely. "That's OK, Son," the Bambino smiled, and gave Tony a quarter tip, a fortune in the 1920's.

Tony resolved never to spend that quarter, revering it like a church relic, "…until the day a great Charlie Chaplin movie came to the Nicolodeon," he laughed.

Thanks to Johnny Martin's training, the two brothers eventually got their licenses, their own place, and enjoyed over 40 years of companionship in Tony and Buster's Barber Shop, a Pittston landmark.

Every Friday morning, Tony's mother baked homemade bread. As a child, I loved Nanna's big cellar stove, where she made huge, round loaves of fragrant Sicilian bread, topped with *giggiulena* (sesame seed) for each of her five married children, with a little round *panino* (roll) for each grandchild. Lovingly wrapping each family's "care package" in a brown grocery bag, she waited for a grandchild from each home, all within walking distance, to come for the bread. If we were late, she delivered it herself. "Be sure to stop at Nanna's for the bread, so she doesn't have to make the trip here," was our Friday warning.

We children were fascinated by Nanna's framed picture of an angel bearing a banner, "In questa casa, non si bestemmia." (In this house, one does not curse.) Your morals and your mouth had to be beyond reproach in Nanna's house.

She not only loved her religion, she lived it! Honesty first! Duty, family, country! Give and never cost the cost. God sees all and God rewards. Help people!

One of the few to survive the Spanish influenza of 1918, she visited homes during the epidemic, cleaning and cooking for her lady friends, and also serving as neighborhood midwife. When Josephine came down with the dreaded illness, Luigi bought his bride the pink medicine prescribed by the American doctor. Nanna knew that her friend Maria had taken the medicine and died from the flu anyway. The same for friends Concetta and Giovanna. She poured a dose of medicine down the sink each day, so Luigi would think she was taking it, and cured herself with hot chicken soup and many rosaries to *la Bedda Madre*, (the Blessed Mother) her best friend, after Jesus, of course.

From then on, there were no doctors for Nanna, not even when she took a tumble down the steep concrete steps leading to her cellar kitchen. Her children insisted that the gash on her forehead needed stitches from a doctor. But Nanna said no, and nothing could move her. Clutching her rosary in one hand, she clamped her wound together with a wet towel held in the other, then prayed non-stop until the two sides of the gash held together, and the bleeding stopped. A scar remained thereafter, but the wound would have left a scar anyway, she reasoned, stitched or unstitched.

Nanna walked to church and baked bread until she was nearly ninety. Never seen in robe or slippers, she lived to be 104 with no illness, no eyeglasses, a keen mind, and legs strong enough to climb the stairs to her second-story bedroom. "I owe it all to Jesus and *la Bedda Madre*," she often said. When she started to walk a bit shakily, she got her first pair of sneakers, size five, to keep her little feet steady on her new kitchen floor.

Grandma never forgot the birthday of any of her grandchildren. It was the custom, upon entering an Italian grandmother's home, to kiss her and say, "*Sa benedica, Nanna*," (Give me your blessing). The answer was, "*Santa*." (May you become a saint.) As she gave you her blessing on your birthday, she would silently tuck a folded bill into the palm of your hand, then pat your hand with a smile.

The door was always open for neighbors to come in for coffee, homemade bread, and a chat. Many asked for prayers, since she loved *L'Addolorata* (our Lady of Sorrows), patron saint of her little Italian village of Serra di Falco, whose statue she followed loyally in procession up and down the hills of Pittston each year on September 15th.

In her 90's, no longer able to march behind *L'Addolorata*, she was honored by our parish, who brought the statue, band, and procession to her house on Pine Street. Out she came, with her Blessed Mother pin attached to her best dress, and her $20 bill to pin on the blue ribbon. "That's too much for a widow," people said. (It was a lot in the 1960's.) "No," she insisted, "That's for all the medicine I didn't have to buy, thanks to *L'Addolorata*." Looking at the statue, she whispered, "*Grazie*. If I'm alive next year, I give you more."

The family had a huge party on Pine Street for her 100th birthday, the President sent a telegram, and our local newspaper came to take her picture for the front page. "Not without my good earrings and my best dress," she insisted. I don't want to look like a *vecchiaredda*." (old lady) A story went around that the photographer had said, "Mrs. Palmeri, it's a privilege to take your picture for your 100th birthday. And I hope to be back again next year for your 101st." Nanna answered, "I don't see why not—you look healthy to me!" Whether this was another one of my Dad's jokes or not, we never found out.

But our all-time favorite story was the New York Subway Miracle of Nanna's youth: After settling their families in Pittston, young Josephine and her three brothers, Joe, Sam, and Leo, sent money to Italy for their mother, Jenny Giarratano, to come to America. On the day of her arrival, Josephine and my three great-uncles went to New York to pick up their beloved mother.

Four unschooled immigrants, who had never been anywhere except their Italian farm village, and the little coal-mining town of Pittston, now took a train for the Big Apple! With their money pinned to their coat linings, and Uncle Sam's broken English, they found their way to the New York subway. Through trial and error, they reached the right platform for the Battery.

Pushed along by the rush-hour crowd, the three brothers were swept aboard the subway car without Josephine, whose tiny frame they could see, desperately trying to enter the closed doors. Three frantic faces at the window watched their panic-stricken sister. "Stop the train!" shouted Uncle Sam, until the conductor came to investigate. "Go back! My sister, she no get on."

"Can't stop now, Mister," said the kind conductor, "but here's what I'll do. Take this transfer ticket. At the next stop, you get off and go back. She'll be there, don't you worry."

Meanwhile, the abandoned Josephine watched horrified as her brothers disappeared into the dark tunnels of the New York subway. Panic overwhelmed the young woman, unable to speak a word of English, watching the crowd rush madly about her, bewildered by the din of strange voices and the roaring of trains. To whom could she turn? Pulling her rosary from her pocket, she dropped to her knees, raised her pleading hands to heaven, and cried in Sicilian to her best friend: "Blessed Mother, help me. I have no one but you. Come down or send an angel to help me." Her loud desperate cries were chanted over and over, like a litany. People gathered around the hysterical young woman kneeling on the platform.

At that moment, another Italian immigrant reached the scene. Drawn by the sound of his Sicilian dialect being chanted in the subway, he followed the voice to a kneeling, crying woman, oblivious to everyone around her. "Josephine, is that you?" he asked in amazement. She opened her eyes to see Cataldo Butera, a neighbor from her home village of Serra di Falco. He had settled in Manhattan, spoke English, and knew all about the subway.

Josephine grabbed his hands and explained her plight. "Don't you worry," he assured her. "Your brothers will get off at the next stop and come back for you. Let's just wait here. I'll stay with you." Josephine dried her eyes and thanked God for sending an angel down from heaven in the form of Cataldo Butera.

Sure enough, in ten minutes, Joe, Sam, and Leo, noses pressed against the train window, reached the platform where Josephine stood, clutching her rosary. What a joyful reunion! This time, the four siblings walked with arms linked like a Roman phalanx, until they arrived safely back home with my Great-grandma Jenny as the fifth link.

Josephine went straight to the Sacred Heart statue in her parlor, knelt in thanksgiving, and made up a short poem-prayer, right on the spot:

"Gesú, Gesú, di Pittston, non nescio chiu!" (Jesus, Jesus, I will never leave Pittston again.) And she never did. Except to travel to Morristown, New Jersey, where I took my vows as a nun many years later. She had kept her promise until age 90, but felt it was OK to leave Pittston just this once. After all, one's granddaughter does not become a nun every day. And anyway, the Blessed Mother would protect her in New Jersey. Hadn't she worked a miracle in the New York subway, just for her?

✂ ✂ ✂ ✂ ✂

GROWING IN LOVE

Dating in the 1930's was strictly chaperoned for Italian-American couples in Pittston, Pennsylvania. My parents were never really "all alone" until their honeymoon. The marriage was first "planned" in the mind of my paternal grandfather, Luigi. Tony's family lived two doors down from my mother's. Luigi Palmeri told his son that Josephine Manganaro would make him an ideal wife: she came from good, hardworking, church-going people like the Palmeris. *"Femina di casa"* (woman of the home), Luigi called her. Tony knew her by sight—she was cute, petite, refined, with a lovely smile, and a peaceful air. Knowing that all men had to get married sometime, he agreed to have his parents "ask for her."

Mr. and Mrs. Palmeri visited the Manganaros to ask if their daughter was interested. Privately consulted by her parents, 19-year-old Josephine said she was too young, not ready for marriage. Mom often told me that she already had been running her sick mother's household: Josephine baked the bread, cooked, sewed, and kept the house spotless. She was like a married woman already, and she was her own boss.

Tony was secretly relieved by the refusal, since at 21, he was not *really* ready to settle down. There were dances to attend at Pittston's Armory Hall where Ozzie and Harriet Nelson once performed, and he enjoyed hanging out with his young, single buddies. "We were an innocent bunch of guys, with curfews, still obeying our strict fathers, and going to Mass every Sunday morning, so "sowing our wild oats" merely meant a few more ball games, dances, and card games without the responsibility of marriage.

Five years later, however, each was ready. The offer was made again, and this time Josephine accepted handsome, hazel-eyed Tony, "the catch of 1935," as she loved to say.

One day the young engaged couple asked Josephine's Dad for permission to go to nearby Rocky Glen Amusement Park, a 12-minute train ride away. The answer? "No...when you're *married* you go to Rocky Glen." The couple was allowed to go together to church, to family gatherings, to a movie downtown, and to visit at Josephine's home. Here they planned the furnishing of their little apartment, on the same street, Mr. Manganaro's rent-free gift to the new couple for one year.

Their first "all-alone" time was dinner in a restaurant on the night of their honeymoon in New York City's Lincoln Hotel. (We still have the bill for their 4-night stay—$16.) Josephine's chicken was a bit tough and hard to cut. Tony, wanting to impress his struggling new bride, grabbed her dish. "Here, Honey, let me cut it." He sawed away so hard, that the chicken slid off the plate, across the table, and a few feet across the floor!

The Italian waiter approached the table with a grin, "What-sa matter? The chicken-a she fly away?" Bride and groom laughed, easing Tony's embarrassment, and another chicken dinner was brought to the table.

After dinner they danced to the top tune of 1935, "It's Three O'Clock in the Morning." Dad loved to tell how they bonded in a beautiful lifetime relationship: "You know, we didn't *fall* in love. We *grew* in love!"

✂ ✂ ✂ ✂ ✂

TONY & PITTSTON: A Mutual Love

"What I love about this little town," Tony often said, "is that everybody in Pittston knows your business. If you have a black eye, you don't have to keep explaining how you got it. They **KNOW** already!

Our mailman <u>really</u> knew everyone's business. He used to read all our postcards. He knew who was on vacation, where they went, and when they'd be back.

Now…we didn't mind him <u>reading</u> the cards, but when he started <u>answering</u> them, we got mad!

Tony loved giving tours of Pittston! Once he took a friend from Texas for a walk:

Tony: Look at our beautiful Pittston Post Office, Tex!
Tex: Hmmm. Our dead letter office is about this size.
Tony: See our Water Street bridge over the Susquehanna?
Tex: Looks like a little Tinker Toy over a stream.
Tony: Let's buy some of these fresh melons.
Tex: Melons? Our **grapes** are that big in Texas.

By nightfall, Tony was fed up with Tex's "bigger and better," so he put three huge snapping turtles in his bed. Tex turned back the covers and screamed, "What in the Sam Hill are <u>those</u>?

Tony said smugly, "Pennsylvania bed bugs!"
Tex paused a moment and said, "Young ones, ain't they?"

✂

Tales from the Barbershop

Tony loved to visit the grocery store of Tillie & Arthur Bullett, our closest friends. One day a child said, "My mother wants six rolls of toilet paper, and please charge it." Tillie bagged the rolls and opened the ledger. Momentarily forgetting the family's name, she asked, "Sonny, who's this for? The puzzled child said, "We're **ALL** gonna use it."

✂

Tillie and Arthur lived across from St. John's Cemetery on Market Street, a pleasant neighborhood. When folks asked, "Aren't they afraid to live near a graveyard?" Tony replied, "Naw! People in the cemetery are good neighbors. They'd never hurt you. With a wink, he'd add, "And they never talk about you behind your back."

✂

Not only did Tony love Pittston-Pittston loved him! Tony and Buster's Barber Shop was a haven for many. Before the Beatles and hippies, men got frequent haircuts. Sofas were there for customers waiting, and for folks who just wanted a friendly place to visit.

Everyone knew the barber shop: judges and janitors, clerks and coal miners, bakers and bankers, kids and senior citizens. People stopped in to say hi, use the phone, get a drink of water, read the paper, or use a restroom. On cold days, folks dropped in to warm up. Tony and Buster's magazines were clean reading for men, women, and kids. The two brothers offered pleasant company, free jokes, and advice. Signs on the wall reflected the Palmeri philosophy:

**"Be nice to people.
They need all the help they can get."
"Be good to the little people on your way to the top-
you'll meet them again on your way down."
"Instead of a kick in the pants, go a little higher
and give folks a pat on the back."**

✂

Children were Tony's specialty. Weary mothers whose tots screamed during haircuts were told, "Take him to Tony's. He has a special technique."

Tony would tie a big striped barber sheet around the child and point to a spot on the kid's tummy. "Keep your eyes here on this spot," Tony would whisper. "There's a little bunny who pops his head up once in a while. But he disappears so **fast**, that if you look away, you'll **miss** him."

The child in the barber chair would gaze with bowed head, watching for the bunny, as Tony trimmed the back of his neck with electric clippers, which the child did not fear, since Tony had already shown him how the clippers sang *ziggety-zig-zig*. Kids looked forward to their next haircut, because, "Maybe the bunny might pop up today!"

Only one little boy ever claimed to "see" the bunny. The child, who must have had an overactive imagination, began to shout, "I saw him! I saw him!" No one else ever saw him, but word spread, and other kids hoped that one day they might see the bunny too.

✂

Although Tony was the great story teller, he liked to praise his kid brother Buster's humor. "I can **tell** jokes," Tony would say, but Bus can make them up." One day, Buster said to a friend making fun of his flashy socks, "Yep, I got *sox* appeal." "See? That's what I mean!" said Tony, in praise of his brother's wit.

✂

When business was slow, Tony looked from his big shop window for friends who might need a ride. Not everyone had cars back then, but everything in Pittston was within walking distance: church, school, and blocks of stores. He would invite ladies to leave heavy packages in the barber shop until they finished their shopping. When they came back for their bags, he'd drive them home if he had no customers.

Tony especially watched for people he knew were in pain, but couldn't afford a car. Many have told me of the times he left his shop to drive them home.

✄

When Sr. Marietta Rosi, MPF, of Mt. Carmel's Convent, William Street, retired to our Motherhouse in New Jersey, she often talked about Dad. "If he saw me through the window, he'd yell, 'Sr. Marietta, I'll drive you up the hill.' If he had a customer, he'd insist I come in and wait. When he finished, he'd take my bags and drive me home."

In her 80's, Sr. Marietta lost her memory, but never forgot Dad's kindness, and repeated it like a broken record. "Did I ever tell you how good your father was to me?" Since Dad had passed away, I loved to hear her tell it again. It "brought him back" for a few minutes.

Sr. Marietta, forgetting I had no license, often asked me to take her out. To my answer, "Sister, I don't know how to drive...remember?" she would scold, "You are **not** like your father! He was kind! If **he** were here, **he** would drive me! Did I ever tell you how he would leave the barber shop and drive me home...?" When nuns asked, "Aren't you tired of that story?" I would reply, "Not **THAT** one."

✄

When Tony's friends were sick, he took his black barber satchel to their homes or the hospital, to provide haircut, shave, jokes and laughter. Nurses knew him by sight and took him to patients who were depressed. "Go in and make them laugh, Tony," they'd whisper. A visit from you is better than medicine."

In April of 1978, the Holy Name Society of St. Rocco's, our parish on Tompkins Street, named Tony "Man of the Year" for the joy he had given the people of Pittston throughout his life.

No one, not even his family, knew he had only **one** month to live. The speeches and tributes were overwhelming. As friends later said, "Tony heard his eulogy while he was still alive."

My mother kept scrapbooks of clippings of his storytelling career and letters of tribute: Here are some excerpts:

"...at the annual St. Rocco's Holy Name Society Smoker on Sunday, April 9...special honored guest for the evening will be **Tony Palma** Palmeri, well-known and loved Greater Pittston barber and humorist. Tony has thrilled us all over the years with his appearances at regional banquets...one of the most sought-after dinner speakers in the region." (*Sunday Dispatch, April 1978*)

"Our honored guest...has been a very active member of the community, both civic and religious. In...the early minstrel shows in St. Rocco's, Tony was a storyteller, and was then on stage for many years, earning a reputation as one of the area's funniest and most professional humorists. It is for this talent of bringing joy and laughter, and his many years of service in the Society that we honor TONY PALMA today." (*"Man of the Year" program booklet, St. Rocco's Church, Pittston, PA, 4/9/78*)

The **Sunday Dispatch** called him "...a special man in Greater Pittston...a local barber for over 47 years and a well-known and loved humorist and athlete. Tony possesses a special gift from God...his ability to make people laugh and smile...no one loved his humor more than our late editor, William A. Watson, Sr." (*Dispatch, February 12, 1978*)

"Dear Tony: Congratulations on being honored as St. Rocco's Man of the Year. You are certainly most deserving of this recognition. ...Kindest personal regards, Arthur" (*From Judge Arthur Dalessandro, Luzerne County Courthouse, Wilkes-Barre, April 1978*)

"Dear Tony…What a beautiful tribute to a man who deserves all the praise that a grateful community has to give. Tony, we have long been aware of your gifted talent as an outstanding barber, but your gift of story telling and your priceless sense of humor is one that God has favored singularly upon you. It must give you much pleasure to be able to bring laughter and happiness into the lives of so many people. You have won the respect and admiration of everyone in the entire area, and you have every right to be proud of the reputation you have earned… It is our sincere hope that God will bless you and your brother Buster, with many more years of good health to continue to service and entertain the people of Pittston. Hoping that Tony's Barber Shop will be around for a long, long, time to come… Frank J. Barbera, President (*Greater Pittston Chamber of Commerce*)

"Dear Tony…Some people tear down-you are a builder. It is a privilege to know you and to serve you. Most sincerely, James VanScoten, Executive Director, Pittston YMCA (*From a letter dated May 9, 1978, 3 weeks before his death*)

"Dear Mrs. Palmeri, It was with deep and profound regret that we learned of the death of your beloved husband, Tony…we want you to know how keenly his loss will be felt by everyone here. Tony Palma had the respect and admiration of everyone who came into contact with him. To few are granted so warm a personality and priceless sense of humor. A deep void has been caused by his untimely passing… Yours most sincerely, Frank J. Barbera, President" 5/31/87 (*Greater Pittston Chamber of Commerce*)

We received tribute to Dad in letters from lawyers, judges, bankers, priests, plus countless others from "ordinary people," a class to which Tony was proud to belong.

Alan Bullett, 14-year-old grandson of dear friends Arthur and Tillie Bullett, sent Dad this letter three days before his death. Like many other children, Alan called him "Uncle Tony."

Here is one section: (original spelling unchanged)

> "Dear Uncle Tony:
>
> I'm very, very sorry to hear that your ill, so I thought I'd write to you and maybe cheer you up a little. You're a great man. I always liked you, ever since I was a little kid. I know I'm not the only one. A great man has a great number of good friends, and you've got 'em. You've always been nice to me, and everyone else. You've always been nice to people, no matter who they are or what they do.
>
> Love, Alan

✂ ✂ ✂ ✂ ✂

EARTHLY FATHER – IMAGE OF GOD?

The class was called *Bible for Teachers.* Sr. André emphasized, "*Never* tell children, 'God is just like your father.' Those with abusive fathers will project all their hostilities, anger, and fears on God."

"How *do* you teach children about God, then?" asked one woman.

Sr. André taped a large sheet of white paper on the chalkboard and printed, **"A Good Daddy."** "You ask the children to tell you what a good Daddy does. Those with good fathers will describe the Daddy they have: 'He tells you nice stories. He takes you for ice cream. He plays games with you.' He laughs when you tell a knock-knock joke.' "

"Those with abusive fathers will describe the daddies they *wish* they had." Sister told of some frightening answers she had received: 'He would never burn you with cigarette butts. He doesn't lock you in the cellar if you break something. He doesn't leave you home all by yourself when it's dark. He doesn't hit your Mommy.' "

Sister explained that she would create categories from each child's answer, printing on the chart: "Would never do anything to harm you. Gives you food and other nice things. Likes to be with you. Will not leave you alone. Treats you and your family with love. Likes to see you happy." "When the flow chart is filled, you sum up, 'Children, God is like **this** good Daddy we just described.' "

That's when I first realized that not every child grew up with parents like mine.

Early in their marriage, Dad told my mother, "Honey, you have the kids all day long, so when I come home from the barber shop, *I'll* get them ready for supper."

We knew Daddy was home by a unique whistle he gave as he climbed our front porch steps at six p.m. Neighborhood children swarmed around him with cries of "Tony's home!" for he often had pockets filled with unsold-but-still-fresh candy from the barber shop, which he preferred to give away rather than hold over for next week. "Look at him—the Pied Piper!" Mom would laugh. "Everywhere that man goes, sunshine follows." Hanging up his coat and hat, Dad began his ritual. After standing me on a chair before the kitchen sink with a large towel around my neck, he would wash my face with a few strokes of his big hand. The towel was then raised to cover my eyes. "Boo!" he'd tease as he dried my face. Then out came the long, thin barber comb, as he parted my hair in one swift stroke, and combed my bangs. Although Tony didn't know the word "bonding," that's what he did each night.

In those pre-TV days, we listened to the radio: Inner Sanctum, Amos and Andy, Lux Presents Hollywood, or we played games on the back porch. Movie Stars was a favorite. "B. C., a boy!" Daddy would say. "Bing Crosby," I'd shout. "Now it's my turn. F.S., a boy!" "Frank Sinatra!" he'd answer. Although he knew many more stars than I did, he always let me win.

Perhaps my first memory of Tony was when I was about three. I was enjoying my bird's eye view high up on his shoulder. A dog trotted near us. Although afraid of dogs, I remember looking down at the animal, thinking, "He can't get me. He can't come up here." I knew I was safe as long as my Father was holding me in his arms. Years later I transferred this image to a loving God. I'm always in His arms, so I'm safe. The devil? He can't get me as long as I'm with my Father." This warm memory floods me with peace. My only sadness is that not all little girls had such a Daddy.

One sweltering hot night when the power went off, he stood at my bedside and fanned me with a big towel until I fell asleep. The flip-flop of the towel as he snapped it in the air was a comforting sound. Again, that peaceful feeling: "Daddy's taking care of everything."

In 1942, air raids were held to practice for an enemy attack. One cold winter night, Dad had just arrived for supper when the sirens began to howl. "An air raid!" Mom exclaimed. "Tony, I'm so glad you're home!" All lights were turned off. Daddy lit a cigarette (he quit smoking later) and sat me on the kitchen table. Although not quite sure what air raids were at age five, I knew we had to be quiet. I felt peaceful and safe in the dark, with both my parents sitting at the table near me. When the all-clear sounded and the lights went back on, Daddy asked, "Were you scared, JoJo?" "No," I said, "I could see the little red light on your cigarette." "Though I walk in the dark valley, I fear no evil, for you are with me." (Psalm 23)

For a great talker, there was one thing Tony **never** said. He never mentioned that he had always wanted a son, nor did he show disappointment in having two daughters. Not even when the *Sunday Dispatch*, in my sister Santina's birth announcement, stated that *another girl* was born to Mr. and Mrs. Tony Palma, with the "brilliant" finale that the popular barber's other daughter, Josephine, was also a girl. Redundant? Yes! But his reporter friends liked to "stick it to him." Hearing Mom and Dad laugh over the write-up, I never knew it was a "put-down."

My parents often bragged, "Wow, do we have two smart girls!" And Dad proudly told how Santina once saved his life by insisting on driving him to a doctor to have some alarming symptoms checked, ignoring his protests that he was OK.

Only once, when I was 33, did I hear his desire for a male heir. In 1971, Tony couldn't wait to give his adored grandson Brian his first haircut. Santina, however, wanted long hair on her toddler and refused to give permission. "You'll scalp him!" she protested. Dad was annoyed when folks would say,

"How cute your granddaughter is!" or "What's the little girl's name?"

"All my life I wanted a boy!" he shouted one day. "Now I finally have one! And my daughter makes him look like a girl!" All his life he wanted a boy? What a revelation! But by that time, he had given me so much unconditional love and self-esteem, that I could take it.

✂ ✂ ✂ ✂ ✂

JOKES IN THE CEMETERY

Tony didn't want his kids to be afraid of death, so he talked about it as casually as the weather, sometimes around the dinner table. One conversation went like this:

Tony: You know, Jo, if I die first, and you meet someone you like, I want you to marry again. I have a lotta friends. At my wake they'll all come to shake your hand. Look 'em over. The ones you like, give their hand a little extra squeeze. Let 'em know you're interested.

Jo: OK, it's nice to have your blessing. Would you mind if I became a nun instead?

Tony: Naw, whatever you want. Once I'm gone, I want you to be happy.

Jo: And I feel the same way. You'd make a wonderful priest, but if you want to remarry, that's good too. You know who's a nice girl, Tony? (Mom mentioned one of the neighbors.) She's pleasant, never married and she's got a lot of money saved up from all her years working in the dress factory. She'd be a good wife!

Tony: Never mind! I'll pick out my own girl. And something else. At the wake, no screaming and crying like the oldtimers used to do. Cheez, they used to put on a show. They thought the louder they ranted and raved, the more it would look like they loved their husbands.

You know, there are two kinds of widows: the <u>bereaved</u> and the <u>relieved</u>. Some of them had rotten husbands. When the bum died, they were <u>relieved</u>, but they had to put on a show of grief, or it wouldn't look good.

And none of this nonsense dressing the kids in black. Or forbidding them to watch TV, or have a Christmas tree. I always hated those old customs. The family's already brokenhearted. If a little music or going to a movie cheers them up, let them do it.

✂

When one of Dad's best friends died, he was brokenhearted, but annoyed at the "rant-and-rave" display of the widow, who kept interrupting the pastor's graveside prayers screaming, "Jim, I won't leave you here!"

"I wish she'd stop that," Dad mumbled to Mother. "Don't you do that when I die, ya hear? Cheez, we feel bad enough without her screaming."

"Shhhh, Tony, be quiet," Mother admonished.

After the fourth piercing scream of "Jim, I won't leave you here!" Dad could take no more." To lighten his grief, he nudged Mother in the ribs, and whispered, "Jo, how much you wanna bet she leaves him here?"

✂

In 1940, wakes were held in the family parlor. Both my grandfathers died that year when I was three. After explaining casually that Grandpa had gone to heaven and we were going to see his body for the last time, Dad carried me into the parlor.

We stood near the coffin for a moment, but I felt no fear. I was in my Father's arms and knew nothing could harm me. Mother had dressed me in my prettiest ruffled frock, and people murmured, "Ah, isn't she sweet?"

Someone gave me a dime. Mother broke off a flower from a floral piece and gave it to me. Lots of company, lots of food, and all this attention. I grew up with the impression that wakes were lovely social events.

Later in life, I transferred this image to a Heavenly Father. As long as we're in His arms, we have nothing to fear.

Dad didn't want us to fear cemeteries either. Our best friends, Arthur and Tillie Bullett lived on Market Street across from St. John's Cemetery. "Aren't they afraid to live across from a graveyard?" someone asked. "Whatta ya mean?" Dad answered. "Those are the best neighbors. They can't hurt ya. They're quiet and peaceful. And they never talk about ya behind your back."

One summer day, he had Mother pack a picnic lunch and took us to eat it in St. John's Cemetery. Sitting high on a grassy hill under a weeping willow, enjoying warm breezes and a colorful panorama of flowers, trees, and statues, we talked, joked, and laughed. After lunch, Dad suggested, "Let's walk around and make poems about the names on the gravestones." Scampering among the stones, 8-year-old Santina saw the name Kelly. "Mr. Kelly, Mr. Kelly, died from a pain in his belly." Dad praised her ability to create instant rhyme. Everyone had a turn, and we came back home totally at peace with ourselves and the world.

Years later I taught several teenagers who confided to me their horror of anything related to death. They had never gone to a wake, and the very word "cemetery" gave them the creeps.

After hearing of my childhood upbringing, fifteen-year-old Rita asked if I would help her conquer her graveyard phobia. We chose the loveliest Spring day of the year, and walked through our nuns' pretty little cemetery, filled with crimson azaleas. I held one of her hands, and her best friend held the other. We were accompanied by fifteen of her classmates, her mother, and Nero, our convent puppy, whom she loved. Trembling, she completed her pilgrimage from one wrought-iron gate to the other. "I did it!" she rejoiced.

Again, I thanked Tony for his gentle wisdom in teaching his girls that death is merely the exchange of earthly life for eternity.

✂ ✂ ✂ ✂ ✂

JOKES ON A DEATHBED

Tony was dying, and he knew it. "My bags are packed, and I'm ready to go," he said, quoting the late Pope John XXIII. For a while, he was able to walk from his hospital room to other patients on his floor, bringing joy wherever he went, with his jokes and down-to-earth spirituality. Mom had often said he would have made a great priest.

Word spread that this man had charisma, a dynamic energy, filling any room he entered with positive vibes. "Tony's better than a medicine," the staff would say. "Send him to cheer up the lady in Room 404; she's had a bad day."

But the myelofibrosis he had fought for several years would claim Tony's life at age 69. Bedridden, and realizing the end was near, he called our pastor from St. Rocco's Church, Father Mario Buttini, to anoint him with the Last Sacraments.

Then he ordered his doctor to remove the tubes causing him so much discomfort. The doctor pleaded, "Tony, you're breaking my heart talking like that! You've given up on me! I've grown to like you so much—and you gave up!"

Tony switched to his gentle Bing Crosby voice. "Doc, I didn't give up. My body gave up! Patting the bed, he said, "Here. Sit down and I'll explain it to ya."

Doctor sat on the bed like a little boy, head bowed, hands between his knees.

"Doc! Nobody's blaming you. You're a good doctor! You done the best you could! But there comes a time in everyone's life when you have to leave this earth, see? And when that time comes, even the greatest doctor in the world can't save you. My time is up, Doc. You're not prolonging my life; you're prolonging my death. I'm begging you: Stop everything that's prolonging my death. OK?" The Doctor nodded.

In came two of Dad's cousins. "Hey, Tony, you look great! Listen, old slugger, the game's not over yet. Bases are

loaded and you're at bat! You won't strike out, Buddy-Boy! You're gonna win this game!" Suddenly, Tony began to moan—loud, spooky moans and groans. The cousins looked uncomfortable. Turning to my Mother they mumbled. "Jo, you think we should leave?" "Maybe that's best," Mom nodded. "Thank you for coming. God bless you."
 As their footsteps faded down the corridor, Tony opened one eye and whispered, "Are they gone?"
 "Oh, you phony!" Mother accused. "I knew those groans were fake."
 "Aw, Honey, I couldn't stand it. I hate when they say I look great and I'll get well. When people come, let's tell the truth: I'm dying and I want to tell them goodbye."
 Mom nodded. "By the way, I saw Joe Graziano today. He wants to see you, but he said sick people fear undertakers visiting the hospital; they're afraid of being jinxed."
 "That's the stupidest thing I ever heard!" Tony sputtered. "Tell my friend Graziano to get in here, and bring his tape measure with him—save himself a trip later! He's going to get the body in a few days anyway."

✂

 It was late, and time to go home. Before we left, Daddy stopped me. "Honey, you're a nun. Please, I want you to say a special prayer—that I'll fall asleep tonight, and wake up in Heaven. OK? Don't pray for a miracle, 'cuz I'll only have to go through this ordeal again next year. Let's get the show on the road, OK?"
 I promised to do as he asked. "Now lemme hear what prayers you're gonna say tonight," he insisted.
 "Daddy, I'll say: 'Lord, into Your hands I commend my Father's spirit. Jesus, Mary, and Joseph, may he breathe forth his soul in peace with you. Dear Lord, let my Father fall asleep tonight and wake up in heaven.'"
 "Ah, that's nice," he smiled. "I like that. You're a nice girl, Josie."

The next morning, as we stood around his hospital bed, Tony began to awake from his sedated sleep, mumbling hopefully, "Did I die? Am I in heaven?" He opened one eye and saw me. His face fell. "Am I still **here**?" he demanded.

"Yes, Daddy," I whispered. "You're in the hospital."

"Aw, sh_t!" he exploded. "What kind of prayers did you say, anyway?'

"Daddy, I prayed that you would fall asleep and wake up in heaven."

"Well, ya done a lousy job!" he spurted, in his Archie Bunker voice. "Cripes, ya send them to the convent, and they can't even pray right! Never mind, I'll say my own prayers!"

Extending his arms, he shouted, "Lord, You said, 'Come to me, all you who labor and are burdened, and I will give you rest.' Lord, I'm burdened, and I'm asking You for rest. I want to die. Come and get me. Please!"

And he died that day. If Death could be called beautiful, Tony's was: surrounded by his wife, daughters, his beloved brother Buster, his sisters, nieces, and nephews, praying around his bed. Aunt Jenny had asked if he wanted us to say the Rosary aloud. He nodded. Shortly after the Rosary, one long peaceful sigh, and it was over.

Father Buttini walked in at that moment. "He's gone, Father," we said.

The old priest gave him a blessing, and kissed his forehead. "Goodbye, my friend." he said.

✂

At my Dad's wake at Graziano's Funeral Parlor on the Pittston Bypass, the visitors kept coming non-stop. There were no lulls where my sister and I could leave the line of people who came to extend sympathy.

I enjoyed most what one little old lady said as she shook my hand: "Sister, Tony wasn't just a man. He was a monument. He was a landmark. In Pittston we always said, 'I'll meet you at Tony's.'

He told me when I went shopping to leave my packages at the barber shop, and he'd drive them to my house when he closed up. And if I was tired, I could sit in the shop and rest. I'm gonna miss him."

When the nuns came from our Motherhouse in Morristown, New Jersey, they had to wait in a very long line to reach the coffin. My friend, Sister Joan, finally approached me and whispered, "Do you know that the line reaches out the door, down the sidewalk, and onto the Bypass?"

The Sisters had seen a car pull up to the funeral home. The driver had called out to the people lined up outside, "Whose wake is this? Somebody famous? The mayor?"

"No, not the mayor," a man in the line replied. "He was our barber."

At the funeral, Father Buttini gave a eulogy based on the song, "Happy the Man." Funeral Director Joe Graziano had printed the lyrics on Dad's holy card. Joanie, the organist, sang it at Offertory, and the priest, line by line, showed the congregation how the song personified Tony, a man who lived his life doing good, not for reward, but because he loved God and he loved people.

Weeks later I regretted that I had not thought of something. We owned a cassette tape of Dad telling jokes at a banquet. How great it would have been to close the service with Tony's dynamic voice, entertaining his friends at his own funeral, with his finest jokes, especially his "grand finale," for which he was famous:

> Each time I pass a church
> I always make a visit
> So when at last I'm <u>carried</u> in,
> The Lord won't say,
> **"WHO IS IT?"**

✂ ✂ ✂ ✂ ✂

ISBN 1-41205131-2